THE 7 CRITICAL
PRINCIPLES OF EFFECTIVE
DIGITAL
MARKETING

Kasim Aslam

Published by Stone Soup Hustler Publications
Scottsdale, Arizona

Copyright © Kasim Aslam, 2017

Visit Kasim Aslam's official website at www.kasim.me for the latest news, book details, and other information or email Kasim at me@kasim.me

Layout by Guido Henkel

ISBN: 978-1542991001

Subscribe to my newsletter to receive free resources, updates and other wicked fun stuff!

www.kasim.me/connect

TABLE OF CONTENTS

INTRODUCTION

SETTING THE STAGE

THIS ISN'T THE BOOK YOU WANT. I HOPE YOU'LL FORGIVE ME FOR BEING SO presumptuous, it's just that, well, I know you. I know you because I am you. I've spent ten years as a digital marketer. That's ten years beating myself in the face with a keyboard trying to get needles to move, prospects to convert, key phrases to rank, ads to engage and Clients to get the hell out of their own way.

The sad irony of my life is that (if I'm being honest) this isn't the book that I want either. I want a book chock full of bite sized, easy to execute on directions, drawn out in crayon. I want a "connect the dots" manual that'll make my campaigns sing like a drunk pop star on karaoke night. I want a magic book entitled "Press This Button" that'll quadruple my ROI with nothing more than a little tweak to a few landing pages.

I want tips, tricks, tactics and hacks that'll make me look like a damn genius. And that's the problem. It's the problem with me, it's the problem with you, it's the problem with our entire industry. We have turned an honest quest for improvement into an addiction to quick fix, flash in the pan, bullshit. So much of what we spend our time on is composed of nothing but digital smoke and mirrors.

So, while this isn't the book that any of us want, it is the book that we desperately need. Yes, I just went batman with it. (Did I mention that I nerd good? Because I do.) For the sake of the integrity of our entire industry, and for the sake of those we serve, it is time that we acknowledge the systemic problem that plagues the personality of our collective psyche. I am hopeful that this is the first step on a long march in that direction.

Now, before I get all "repent you sinners," let me just say that I love what we do. I LOVE it. Greek style, full bore, out in the open, orgies in the city center, love. We are the gatekeepers of success for the entire business world, a fact that is quantifying in truth with every passing day. And let me tell you something: if you don't believe that, if you don't believe that digital marketers are the new entrepreneurial vanguard, you are in the wrong industry.

I'm not being dramatic when I say that our position in the machine of the global economy is among the most vital in existence. This is especially true for small enterprises—businesses that don't have the same margin of error that very large organizations enjoy. We hold the key to the very survival of the single most important economic demographic in existence and it's time we start taking that position very, very seriously.

The first step to taking it seriously is to begin looking at digital marketing as a discipline unto itself instead of an amalgamation of smaller proficiencies. We are strategists, not button pushers. We are leaders, not order takers. We should be prescribing solutions, solving problems and intuiting whole new worlds of innovation. Instead, we too often stand on the fringe of the battlefield, taking absent minded and impetuous orders from misappropriated generals too encumbered in the thick of battle to understand their mistake in sidelining their most valuable resource.

Here's the thing–it's not their fault–they don't know any better. They don't know any better because they haven't been shown any better. The onus of responsibility to educate those we serve on what (and where) our role is, rests entirely on our shoulders. In order to take up the mantle of strategic leader in place of misused tactician, we need to look at ourselves and what we do differently.

IMPORTANCE OF DIGITAL MARKETERS

MY FATHER IS AN IMMIGRANT. HE CAME TO THE UNITED STATES FROM Pakistan when he was 19 years old. For as long as I can remember, my Dad has marveled at the depth of opportunity available to those of us blessed enough to live in a free Country. I'll spare you the patriotic, 'Merica tirade; just suffice it to say that my Dad loves it here. He's as American as anyone I've ever met and deeply proud of our national heritage.

While Pakistan has its own elements of beauty, I don't think anyone from either country would argue that there's a playing field we've developed in this country that is, as much as it can be, relatively open. While money and influence help (understatement of the century) we're consistently met with story after story of people coming from nothing and achieving impressive entrepreneurial success.

My father started selling baskets door to door in Albuquerque, New Mexico to pay his way through college. He would go on to open his own import/export company and ultimately began selling handmade rugs. His entrepreneurial journey wasn't an easy one. We were never wealthy and experienced our share of struggles. But my Dad never gave up. Today he owns the largest and most respected rug store in Arizona: Alyshaan Fine Rugs.

My Dad isn't a millionaire. He probably could have been by now, but when you peer behind the veil of my father's finances, you'll find something that he doesn't like many people to know (sorry pop). He gives it all away, and I mean he gives everything. My Dad has been supporting an entire extended family in Pakistan for 30 years. He has helped friends, employees, suppliers, family members and strangers. He gives incessantly to causes of the heart like Smile Train and Christian Children's Fund.

My Dad lives in a nice but modest home. He drives a Hyundai that's paid off and well cared for. He doesn't have the things that most of us have been conditioned to look for as indicators of massive success. He has however, been equipped to live the life he set out to live and was able to create this reality for himself through his business. My father's giving has been fueled by his business. Even with the lean times, near misses and disastrous failures, my Dad has built an opportunity for himself to do what matters most to him: to help others and leave the world a better place than he found it.

For those of us who grew up with friends and family that relied on small business for our livelihood, we know how vitally important it is as an institution. Small businesses are the great equalizer of the economic playing field. I'm not saying that it's easy (we all know it's much the opposite); what I am saying is that it's possible. And that possibility surrounds us every single day.

Jim Younger started his construction business with zero capital and a Karmann Ghia, an ugly sedan. He didn't even have a truck! Younger Brothers just celebrated 40 years in business, owns almost a dozen companies, has employed as many as 2,000 people and is currently one of the largest family owned businesses in the Southwest. Mr. Younger also happens to be one of the best men I know.

Ron Turley, who worked at UPS as a fleet manager, saved the company over $100 million by building out systems and procedures for effective fleet management. Ron would go on to start RTA Fleet, a leading fleet management software organization. RTA Fleet is now run by Josh Turley, Ron's grandson.

Tom Veatch started Veatch Ophthalmic Equipment in 1988. Almost 30 years later, the company enjoys one of the best reputations in the industry as an ophthalmic equipment provider. Tom's daughter, Kyna, is now the President of the company which continues to see growth year after year.

Mike Parker started out as a route truck driver for Frito Lay in the low income district of the Washington, D.C. market. He went on to launch his own firm, Next Phase Enterprises, which just celebrated its 20th anniversary. Mike's company represented one client in 1995 and did $4 million in sales. Today his company is a national leading sales and marketing firm specializing in food and beverage programs at the world's largest retailers. They represent over 35 clients today and achieved over $1 billion in retail sales in 2016.

In 1959 Sara (Buckner) O'Meara and Yvonne (Lime) Fedderson opened what would become ChildHelp, one of the oldest and most respected child advocacy nonprofits in the world. In fact, it was through the encouragement and hard work of Sara and Yvonne that April was designated "National Child Abuse Prevention Month" by President Jimmy Carter.

Each of these organizations is a Client of mine. Please understand, I take absolutely no credit for any of what I've outlined above. They were successes long before I met them and would have continued their success regardless of who ended up handling their digital marketing needs.

I bring them up because I want to make a case for why we do what we do. Digital marketing isn't just for big brands. In fact, I contend that larger organizations have a more difficult time with the medium. Digital marketing elevates the organic and grass roots and exposes the mass marketed and contrived messaging.

As a digital marketer, my passion is helping companies like those I've mentioned above. For the ones that have already found their voice, I want to help them build to even greater success. For the ones that are still getting started or have yet to find a solid foothold, I want to be there as a support and launching mechanism. Digital marketing is the secret weapon in the arsenal of global small business.

As a trained warrior with the ability to wield this powerful weapon, it is imperative that you do so responsibly and in a way that helps push our collective agenda forward. I don't mean to say that you shouldn't take the big pay days. You absolutely should! Use them to help position yourself with a level of security that enables you to then spend a little extra time with your smaller Clients.

I've worked with massive organizations, national and international companies with big names and recognizable brands. And yes, when I'm writing a book or doing a speaking engagement, I do the shameless name dropping thing because I'm insecure enough to think I need that type of social proof as reinforcement. When I work for companies like this, I work just as hard as I would for any other Client but these companies aren't the reason I'm in the business.

I'm in business to help small business. If you haven't seen it, there's a meme I love that makes the occasional rounds:

"When you buy from a small business, you are not helping a CEO buy a third vacation home. You are helping a little girl get dance lessons, a little boy get his team jersey, a mom or dad put food on the table, a family pay a mortgage, or a student pay for college."

That same thing is true when you work for a small business. If you're going to read and benefit from this book I'd like to task you with a challenge in return. Regardless of how successful we get, we can't forget the small business. For all of us have been the kid who needed a team jersey, the parent trying to put food on the table, or the student trying to pay for college. We need to make sure we stay true to our roots.

As digital marketers, I hope we can all agree that one of our core values is helping people. People before profits, always. And one of the best ways I know to help people is to help small business. Hopefully you'll pardon this small and slightly dramatic tangent. Dramatic or not, it's something I'm passionate about and a mantle I'm eager to see other people pick up.

WHO IS THIS BOOK FOR?

I'M WRITING THIS FOR PROFESSIONAL DIGITAL MARKETERS. THAT'S NOT TO say you should jump ship if you're not a digital marketer. Business owners & entrepreneurs, agency owners, single focus practitioners (i.e. SEOs, content writers, etc.) and marketing managers, will all greatly benefit from learning *The 7 Critical Principles of Effective Digital Marketing*. In fact, if you're responsible for, or frequently engage with, a digital marketer or digital marketing team, I think this is essential reading in order for you to truly understand the practice.

I make the distinction as to who this is for in order to let you know that I'm going to be making some assumptions. I'm not going to be defining core concepts or explaining what I would expect to be common knowledge facets of digital marketing. I'm doing this for several reasons–the most obvious being expediency. The value I'm here to provide isn't in refreshing anyone's foundational understanding of digital marketing. The 7 Critical Principles are meant to establish a foundation on which the practice of digital marketing can be built.

In fact, defining core concepts would actually work against my ability to establish a digital marketing baseline. Because our industry is so diverse, there's very little in the way of commonly accepted definitions of anything. I have seen things as simple as glossary terms spark semantic arguments that have shattered friendships and sparked bloody nerd wars. Everyone's understanding of what I would call "core concepts" differs from person to person and usually has an extremely heavy bent in the direction of each digital marketer's primary proficiency or vertical.

A sales funnel for a digital marketer who focuses on paid ad management is going to be a lot different than a sales funnel for a digital marketer whose primary emphasis is in email marketing. I'm not here to take sides or split hairs. In fact, I believe this lack of standardization is even more of a reason our industry needs to embrace the axiomatic principles that I outline in this book. Where we will never find a static approach to any of the core concepts digital marketing covers, we can, and absolutely should, work to strengthen our understanding of foundational principles that can transcend implementation and guide our strategic paradigms.

If you have a basic knowledge of digital marketing core concepts, you should have no issue with the concepts presented in this book. If you encounter a topic that is new to you, I would recommend that you stop and perform a few minutes of research before charging forward. Oftentimes you'll find any knowledge gap to be nothing more than an issue of semantics; where I use one word, you understand the same concept by another name. Where I use Avatar, you might understand the same concept as buyer persona or target demographic. And my digital marketing purists are already mad at me and yelling into their Kindle screens that the three aren't the same. Do you see why we can't have nice things?

I'm also assuming that you have at least a cursory knowledge of core digital marketing proficiencies like SEO, PPC, Marketing Automation, Email Marketing, etc. Please keep in mind, you do not need to be experts or even practitioners of any of these from an "in the trenches" perspective. You do however need to understand, on a high level, what they are, what they are used for and (in some cases) how they relate to other proficiencies.

Digital marketers tend to specialize in a handful of proficiencies, and rightly so. Given this reality, I'll also do my best to bring the principles into context for a handful of the broad areas of practice. Hopefully this contextualization will further serve to support the learning process and enable you to apply these principles in your day to day practices.

THE 80%

ON THE NOTE OF "WHO THIS IS FOR," I'M WRITING FOR THE 80%. THIS WAS a difficult but necessary decision birthed from several drafts that were riddled with asterisks, qualifiers and fine print. Here's what I mean: the examples, recommendations for implementation and overall approach will apply to much of the digital marketing world. But, as with anything, there's going to be a minority (20%, if Pareto is to be believed) that operates in a unique or slightly unconventional paradigm.

Trying to qualify every facet of this book with statements like "this applies to most digital marketers" or "while exceptions exist" or "in the vast majority of cases" makes for a laborious read and detracts from the point of the narrative. The principles stand alone and stand strong. I believe they'll survive the test of any qualification one might throw at them. For that reason, I'm not going to try and dance around the specific examples or implementation approaches I provide.

EVERYTHING YOU'RE ABOUT TO READ IS STOLEN...

...BUT POINTING IT OUT MAKES IT OKAY.

I don't really believe that I wrote this as much as I compiled it. The 7 Critical Principles aren't anything that I came up with; they're the natural governing laws of digital marketing. I just pulled them together in what I hope is an easy-to-imbibe format. This is the result of more than a decade's worth of notes, life lessons, mistakes, crushing failures, blinding successes, insane amounts of information and, far more to the point, other people's stuff.

This leads me to a relatively big and necessary disclaimer. Most of these concepts are things that I have learned from someone else. I like to think that I've put my own twist on the way they're articulated and, in some small cases, maybe even implemented. But as a practice and study, they are all borrowed thought–children birthed from the brains of men and women far more intelligent than I.

Where possible, I have given credit where credit is due. Far more often, however, I have no idea where the credit belongs. While on my life's quest of digital marketing knowledge I have collected content, thoughts, opinions and ideas and, like most of us, I tend to assume ownership of these without always attaching the appropriate attribution to them when I file them away in my mind palace. This is mostly because my mind palace is more of an abandoned crack house.

This compilation has been impacted by friends, associates, clients, vendors, employees, authors, speakers, bloggers and other digital marketers. Please don't misunderstand me, there's nothing about what I'm writing that has been plagiarized or (in my view) unethically utilized. Everything I'm writing is of my own mind. I just want to pay homage to the foundational knowledge that put it there in the first place.

So, to those that have helped me build this library of knowledge: I thank you with humble sincerity. Not only have you contributed to this book, you have also contributed to my professional development and my ability to do what I love. So, thank you.

WHAT QUALIFIES ME

WHENEVER YOU CREATE CONTENT, YOU NEED TO ESTABLISH SOME LEVEL OF authority, i.e., the "why you should listen to me" section. I hate this part because I just don't know how to strike the right balance between:

a. The humble expert, gently putting forth his breadth of experience to convince you of his competence and...

b. The narcissistic douche bag, pounding his tribal tattooed chest, sending you pictures of himself standing in front of his (probably leased and soon to be repossessed) Ferrari.

Well, I don't have a bunch of selfies at my San Diego beach house or the too-candid-to-be-real snapshots of me cozying up with a pile of celebrities.

What I do have is well over ten years as a successful digital marketer. I have worked with over a thousand organizations from micro-businesses and startups to Fortune 500 companies and Global NGOs. If you're interested in learning more about me, please visit my website: kasim.me.

The short version of the longer story is that I know what I'm doing. I've been in the digital marketing game since well before it was cool and I have quite a bit in the way of real world experience. If the saying "those that cannot do, teach" holds any merit, I hope you'll view me as one of the ones that do ...do's? does? You know what I'm trying to say.

WHAT DIGITAL MARKETING IS NOT...

BEFORE DISCUSSING WHAT DIGITAL MARKETING *IS*, I FIND IT NECESSARY TO define what digital marketing is not:

Digital Marketing Is Not Selling

Sales is a direct and necessary result of effective digital marketing. However, effective digital marketing should always seek to establish a relationship before a sale is ever made. Effective digital marketing also does not ever compromise a relationship for a sale.

The strange and cyclical logic employed here is this: people and organizations seek to use digital marketing to assist them in boosting sales. However, only those who seek to build relationships through digital marketing will realize the full potential of the sales process.

Don't look at sales as an afterthought. That's just as big a mistake as making it the focus. Instead, look at relationship building as a transcendent manifestation of sales. A sale is a single, isolated transaction with a finite and temporary value. A relationship is an ongoing engagement with limitless potential and compoundable, if not infinite, value.

Digital Marketing Is Not Branding

People may confuse the concept of relationship building with branding but they are two completely different things. Hence, digital marketing is not branding. There's absolutely nothing wrong with branding and it can be an extremely effective practice if executed appropriately.

Branding is the act and process of developing a unique and identifiable entity that consumers can easily identify and engage with. Digital marketing (relationship building) is the act of catalyzing and amplifying the quality of that engagement in a way that creates a lasting connection.

Branding is designing your house so it's pleasant and welcoming. Relationship building is inviting people over to your home for dinner, getting to know them, working to understand who they are on a personal level and then cultivating a lifelong friendship built on a foundation of reciprocity of value.

Digital Marketing Is Not Advertising

Advertising is a push. Digital marketing is (usually) a pull. We'll talk more about the push/pull paradigm in subsequent sections. For now, suffice it to say that advertising is the attempt to interrupt someone else's agenda by pushing your own in front of them. Digital marketing is the practice of working to carefully align your agenda with that of your target prospect so they are synergistic and mutually beneficial.

As with "analog" relationship building, digital marketing needs to "seek first to understand and then to be understood." (Covey 1989) Advertising as a stand-alone practice is the quest to be seen and heard; it's a selfish endeavor meant to stroke egos and built on the assumption that your offering is applicable to the needs of a target consumer base regardless of situation, context or buying cycle.

Obviously, there's a time and place for advertising. In fact, it can be used as a tool within the walls of the digital marketing machine to great effect given the proper execution. But, as a strategy unto itself, advertising is the weak and rotting stick attempting to parade around the forest as an oak tree. Or something like that. No one ever said you had to come up with perfect analogies to be a great digital marketer.

WHAT DIGITAL MARKETING IS...

WHEN I GOOGLE THE DEFINITION OF MARKETING, I GET THIS:

> The action or business of promoting and selling products or services, including market research and advertising. (Webster's Dictionary, 1869)

Blah, blah, blah. Webster can eat dried feces and die.

Digital marketing is relationship building. While that might be a slight over-simplification, I'm going to stand by this definition and fight to the death to defend its sanctity and honor with the stubbornness of a petulant child. To be more descriptive, digital marketing is building a relationship with a prospective Client over a period of time through appropriate and varied channels. This relationship building is accomplished using contextualized content.

Everything we do in the realm of digital marketing is an act of relationship building. Creating awareness, establishing thought leadership, catalyzing action, engaging a user base, collecting followers and aggregating a database, these are all acts of relationship building. This is a "front-facing" definition of course. The backend of digital marketing includes the processes, procedures, and measurement of the practice but done within the confines of the core purpose which is to build relationships.

Relationship building is an absolutely essential paradigm to assume if one is to become an effective digital marketer. This is the understanding that the 7 Critical Principles of Effective Digital Marketing are built on. Relentless and continuous focus on relationship building is paramount and something worthy of constant focus if we are to be consistently successful.

CONTENT + CONTEXT = RELATIONSHIP BUILDING

THE MORE APPROPRIATE YOUR CONTEXTUAL TARGET AND THE MORE compelling your content, the more successful your marketing. This has always been true. The reason digital marketing is so far removed from analog marketing is because the recent shifts in technology and consumer behavior have so drastically altered the way we engage (context) and what we engage with (content).

A single change to one of the two pillars (content and context) would cause a drastic shift, without question. However, what we have in the new digital age is a complete change to both which has caused a collapse of traditional methods. The placement of power in the hands of the consumer has forced marketers to yield to the wants and needs of those they serve. In a really interesting way, this new shift has catalyzed a movement in marketing toward transparency, value and integrity.

PUSH VS. PULL

YOU'LL NOTE THAT THE TITLE OF THIS LITTLE PIECE OF BRILLIANCE ISN'T "The 7 Critical Principles of Effective Marketers." There is a "Digital" in there for a reason. Digital Marketing is different. It's harder, smarter and more effective.

Digital Marketing isn't solely a change of context; it is, instead, a complete change of paradigm. The state and nature of consumer engagement has changed completely. People do not engage with brands, messaging or advertisements the same way they used to. Technological advancements have placed all the power of engagement in the hands of the user.

Marketers used to have the ability to "push" their messaging. They could literally force feed their advertisements *en masse* with little to no repercussion. Television commercials were delivered two, three and four at a time and consumers had no other option than to sit down and take it all in. Radio advertisements enjoyed almost as much real estate as the songs they relied on for viewership. News-paper ads were sought out and people were still catalyzed to action by roadside billboards.

That push messaging approach of yore is dead. We now have the ability to engage with media freely and completely on our terms. We watch television shows on demand. Music is freely available at our fingertips down to the song we want to listen to. News is compartmentalized and provided according to our customized interests. Nobody sees the roadside billboards because they're far too busy texting and driving; sad but true.

Now I know what you're thinking: there are still ads in each one of those examples. Sure, there are. But they're cautiously inserted at far fewer intervals and with a level of targeting that attempts to mitigate the risk of losing or alienating users. User engagement is so coveted that networks have gone as far as adding a countdown timer to their ads. They let you skip ads that aren't relevant and even ask for ongoing feedback regarding the ads they put in front of you.

We used to purchase consumer attention wholesale. Now we're fighting for mere seconds (literally) and paying a commoditized premium for the privilege. The amount of media available and the willingness of other content creators to give it away for nothing more than the whisper of a promise of potential future engagement, has saturated the market to such a degree that it has all but rendered it meaningless.

PRINCIPLES DEFINED

WEBSTER'S DICTIONARY DEFINES PRINCIPLES AS:

> **prin·ci·ple** \'prinsəpəl \ *n* : a fundamental truth or proposition that serves as the foundation for a system of belief or behavior or for a chain of reasoning

And I'm sorry about what I said earlier, Webster. I didn't mean it.

Principles are core truths. They are the foundational concepts upon which we build our beliefs about anything and everything. Principles are not strategies, tactics or even habits. They are far more fundamental than that. Principles are the unchanging and unyielding axioms of any belief or system.

In the realm and practice of digital marketing, as with all industries, there are a myriad of principles that help to make up our industry. While I'm not claiming that the 7 Critical Principles I have outlined in this book are the only principles that are ever present, I do contend that they are the foundational principles necessary for a complete and holistic undertaking of digital marketing as a proficiency.

These principles are meant to influence every other facet of our practice. They should dictate our paradigms and inform our actions. They should be the foundation for our strategic decisions and qualify our tactics. These principles are the guiding light of an effective and successful digital marketer.

The beauty of these principles is that they are the unflinching and unchanging cornerstones of an otherwise elusive and ever-changing industry. It doesn't matter what happens within the realm of digital marketing; as long as the industry survives, so too will these principles. A new tool can launch and take market share tomorrow, and you'll find the application of these core principles just as relevant. I know this because it's happened time and again since the advent of the internet.

In an industry that is changing faster than any industry before it, one that changes at a rate and with a force that is impossible for any one person to control or even fully grasp, it is absolutely essential to our survival that we seek out that which is constant and dedicate ourselves to its study. These 7 principles are exactly that. They are the constants within the storms of change.

CROSSING THE LINES OF PROFICIENCY

As a professional digital marketer, you are more than likely a specialist in one, or maybe even a handful, of digital marketing proficiencies. Even the most well-rounded practitioners tend to focus on specific service verticals. In fact, my experience has been that most digital marketers started as focused practitioners, offering a single service that began to expand by necessity. I started my career building software; software segued to website development which opened the door to organic search marketing. I'm willing to bet you have a very similar story.

Interestingly, when you earn the trust of a Client in a specific vertical of digital marketing, they begin to push other digital marketing requests in your direction. Typically, this push happens regardless of you or your company's prowess in that arena. I have been placed in situations where Clients are all but begging me to take over an initiative or set of initiatives that aren't even within our service wheelhouse. This is the sole reason my agency produces animated videos! People wouldn't stop asking me for them.

This is an important discussion because, even though we have defined (albeit in loose terms) what digital marketing is, we have not defined what a digital marketer is. Where digital marketing is relationship building, a digital marketer is anyone who uses digital tools to facilitate that practice. Digital marketers are relationship builders; the tools you use to execute on that practice are entirely up to you. You can include and exclude them at will; and you can be as clear or as vague about your toolset as you choose.

Every digital marketer (and every digital marketing agency) is different. You might be a focused practitioner with a single, core service offering and ancillary services built around it as a supporting mechanism. For instance, you could be a pay-per-click company that offers conversion optimization and basic nurture campaigns. Or, you might be more of a full-service agency, offering website development, content creation, marketing automation, funnel development, social media marketing, email marketing and SEO. Or, more likely, you offer some combination of the services mentioned above and some additional services that I haven't touched on.

In terms of how you can and should relate to the material presented in this book, your practice verticals are secondary to the 7 Critical Principles. That's not to say that they don't matter. You'll find that every single individual practice will require its own interpretation of the principles. This is true in order to properly contextualize the principle's usage as well as to amplify its value. Said another way, you're going to have to learn how to apply these principles to your own specific approach to digital marketing. I can't offer a standard roll out because, as we just described, every agency and practitioner is unique.

However, these principles apply to every facet of digital marketing regardless of utilization or positioning within your core proficiencies. That's the point I'm trying to make. For you to receive the most benefit from this book, it's important to put aside your perceptions and your prejudices with regard to specific digital marketing practices. As with all axioms, the principles are not meant to be applied to your proficiencies. Instead, your proficiencies are to be built with these core and critical principles woven into their existence.

When you understand the 7 Critical Principles of Effective Digital Marketing, your ability to learn and manage digital marketing practices is quantified on an exponential scale. You'll begin to see immediate benefits to learning the core principles and integrating them into your paradigm and workflow. One of those benefits is the amplification in your ability to scale and grow your business. Where learning a new skill is akin to reading a book, learning the core principles is akin to first learning how to read. It equips you with an understanding that can be applied to all future digital marketing initiatives.

Understanding the 7 Critical Principles will also place you in a position to amplify your own value as a strategic driver. A good digital marketer should drive the direction of every facet of his or her digital marketing campaigns. This is true regardless of whether or not you are performing the actual work. In many cases, you'll be placed in positions that require you to engage with (and possibly even directly manage) your clients' employees, vendors and other providers.

In instances like this, where you're placed in a position to manage a practice that is not your core proficiency, you can trust in your ability to adequately drive any practice related to or contributing to the core digital marketing initiatives. You do so by making sure you're employing the 7 Critical Principles.

These are universal principles in the realm of digital marketing and, if you let them, they'll act as guiding lights in every single strategic initiative of which you are part. Not only will they amplify the value of your existing offerings and equip you to manage other digital marketing channels, they will also make it easier for you to integrate new and varied channels into your core business. This ability to drive and manage offerings that aren't your core proficiency places you in the position of proverbial quarterback on the field of digital marketing success. The value of such a skill can't be overstated.

Remember, digital marketers are never sole practitioners. A core tenet of digital marketing is the ability to amplify value through synergy and synergy can't exist without the ability to compound value. The very nature of digital marketing requires that every initiative integrate and maintain continuity with the overarching digital strategy. Without the ability to coordinate and manage multiple tools in the digital marketing tool belt, you leave yourself ill-equipped as a digital marketer. Learning and applying these critical principles mitigates that risk and positions you for long-term growth and thought leadership with any Client or organization.

CHARACTER ETHIC VS. PERSONALITY ETHIC

IN 1989 STEPHEN COVEY PUBLISHED HIS NOW FAMOUS "THE 7 HABITS OF Highly Effective People." As you'll be able to tell from my title, I was inspired by Covey's format. I say "inspired" simply so I don't get sued. In truth, I have blatantly stolen it with the infantile glee that comes with the emulation of one's heroes.

The title and structure isn't the only facet of Covey's work that I have "borrowed." Covey's explanation as to why he wrote his book is an extremely close representation of why I wrote my own. His examination of character ethic vs personality ethic is something I see reflected pervasively in our industry.

Stephen Covey spent a career studying 200 years of American success literature. He noticed a trend as he moved through the time-line of human achievement. Where the content produced in the past tended to focus on core principles and foundational concepts, there was a marked shift in the approach as he began looking at content being produced closer to his present day.

He called this the shift between the character ethic and personal-ity ethic. The character ethic focused on the idea that personal achievement was advanced based on the nature of one's character. To grow as a person, you needed to exercise the various facets of your character. Covey notes this as being the main idea expressed in the United States up until around World War I.

Around this time Covey found that, at least in mainstream litera-ture, there was a large shift away from character ethic to what he called personality ethic. This shift was manifested in an increasing focus on short-cuts and quick ways to manipulate people or situa-tions to get what one wants. Our misguided need for fast results turned into a focus on the quickest and easiest path instead of taking the time to build the strongest and longest-lasting foundation.

I believe that this same misalignment of focus exists in the realm of digital marketing. The character ethic of digital marketing is abso-lutely alive and well. There are an amazing number of marketers that act upon, and practice, principle-centered marketing on a regu-lar basis. However, our focus as an industry has never been on the principles of marketing, which is to say the "character ethic" of our industry.

Instead, our focus is very clearly on the personality ethic. Almost every single piece of media produced on the topic of effective digi-tal marketing tends to veer in the direction of tips, tricks and hacks to get the fastest results in the shortest amount of time. The appeal of this type of content is obvious and, in many cases, the tactics pro-vided tend to be effective—at least inasmuch as they can be consid-ering how short lived these "tactics" tend to be.

Here's a specific example: HubSpot, a company that produces a lot of excellent content on the topic of digital marketing, put out an article that included the following pro-tip:

Using the word "video" in an email subject line boosts open rates by 19%, click-through rates by 65% and reduces unsubscribes by 26%. (hubSpot.com n.d.)

The personality ethic approach to this type of information is what? We need to add the word "video" to all our subject lines! Have the new intern throw together a quick video and we'll plug that into our next email. Open rates will go through the roof, profits will soar and we'll be heroes.

If you've been in the world of digital marketing for at least 48 hours, you probably have a dozen or so examples of this exact type of thinking. While it seems absurd when you examine it from the outside looking in, this is the exact mentality of our entire industry.

I'm not saying that these data aren't valuable. What I'm saying is we're mistaking where the value resides. The fact that using the word "video" in your email subject line increases open rates simply means that people are more likely and maybe even eager to engage with videos.

However, if we approach this piece of information from the paradigm of the character ethic, it should be obvious that the video we're using needs to be relevant and engaging. It needs to provide value and speak to our prospects' specific needs, hopefully on a segmented level. Sadly, there's far more lip service given to this paradigm than there is tangible action.

When we approach digital marketing through the lens of the personality ethic, we actually work to destroy our own industry. That very statistic (which HubSpot quoted in an article written in 2016) was already two years old according to their own citation. It came from a 2014 article from Syndacast. (Syndacast, 2014)

So, in 2014, using the word "video" in a subject line boosted open rates. How long do you think that lasted? Because as soon as they published results like this, I'm sure a million marketers started pumping out crappy videos just to trick users into opening their emails. This did nothing but acclimate users to the tactic and hurt our ability to use videos to amplify the value of an email.

Take some time and start to look through the content networks that you frequent. I promise you that you'll notice a very glaring trend. Regardless of how well respected these networks are, they've been pulled into the trap of personality ethic approaches.

The content being produced for digital marketers on how to *do* digital marketing (anything from SEO and PPC to conversion optimization and funnel development) is almost solely built around quick win hacks instead of principle-centered approaches. This isn't a condemnation of the creators of this content. They're creating the content that they've seen convert the most effectively; we as marketers are far more likely to consume the quick fix content.

In a way, this is our fault as practitioners. The content that we seek out and actively engage with is the personality ethic content. Content creators are rewarded for giving us what we're more likely to engage with so our interest in quick fix approaches has defined the narrative of an entire industry.

This is the shift that we need to bring about in our own psyche as well that of our industry. There's absolutely nothing wrong with pro-tip content. The hacks and tricks can be great tools to use to amplify campaigns, solve problems and elevate your approach to the next level. However, it is vitally important that these tactics sit atop a solid foundation of strategy. The character ethic of digital marketing needs to be the building blocks of everything we do. The rest of the "stuff" becomes icing on our digital cakes.

IMPACT OF CHARACTER ETHIC

THERE IS NO ROOM IN THE REALM OF DIGITAL MARKETING FOR THAT WHICH is disingenuous. Sales cycles are too long, funnels are too deep and exposure is too great to make any attempt at veiling the truth of an offering. Digital marketing has placed all the power firmly in the hands of the consumer and has acted as the great equalizer in the realm of trade and commerce. The value of the Character Ethic has been amplified due to the transparency that the online medium has created.

Digital marketing has brought about a level of transparency that enables users to educate themselves on everything there is to know about an industry, company, and product or service before they ever have to engage with a salesperson. There has been a gold rush on truth in every industry. Earning the attention of a prospect usually requires being willing to not only give away the secret sauce, but also expose the flaws of your industry and let people peek at your dirty laundry.

This is something that a lot of organizations have a hard time with, especially those that have been operating "the old way" for so long. There used to be a way to ease prospects through the buying cycle, while slowly and strategically introducing them to any potential negatives; all at a pace and in a sequence that allowed the business to manage the flow and narrative of the sales process.

That's gone now. Digital marketing has placed us in a position where all the information is out and on the table. In the earliest days of digital marketing, this was a slower process. In fact, you might remember quite a few organizations attempting to operate under the old paradigm of "prospects are on a need to know basis." However, organizations quickly learned that in order to attract and keep the attention of their users, they need to engage them with increasingly compelling value.

The manifestation of that value in the realm of content marketing is truth. People began telling the truth. I'm not saying that they were lying before. I'm simply saying that they weren't giving the whole truth up front. And yeah, some of them were lying.

Every industry has been commoditized to a degree. Regardless of the product or service you sell, you are in a position where you are marketing to a user base that, in the span of a few seconds, can have a dozen of your competitors up on their screen. From their smartphones, prospects can instantly see comparative pricing, testimonials, features and contract terms. They can make a side-by-side comparison without ever having to engage with you or even express interest.

Entire industries have been built around informing and educating consumers on how to purchase. Prospects can find third party networks dedicated to doing nothing more than objectively comparing your offering with that of a dozen of your competitors. They have access to an endless amount of content, some user generated and some supplied directly from industry professionals. This includes content on how to purchase, the potential points of risk, industry secrets, what questions to ask, what the salesperson doesn't want you to know, and so on.

There is no hiding. Anyone who tries is going to learn the hard way that (once again) the user has all of the power. As a digital marketer, you have to believe in what you are marketing to a degree that you're willing to outline and/or illustrate any potential negatives up front and still expect the value you're offering to exceed the impact of the negative qualifier. If you don't have that level of confidence, then you shouldn't be marketing that product or service.

In fact, this is one of the very first litmus tests I like to use when deciding to take on a new Client. One of the questions I'll ask is: "What are the complaints your customers have about your industry/product/service?" Very rarely do seasoned business owners not have an immediate stream of answers to this. And, if you feel like they're holding anything back, that is often a good reason to at least raise a flag in your mind as to whether or not this is the right Client for you.

Sometimes the answers are simple: the price is high compared to alternatives, turnaround time can be stretched based upon certain factors, long-term contracts are required because [whatever]. Sometimes they're more complex and industry specific. To use an example from our industry: SEO is a service that seeks to optimize a Client's online presence against an ever-changing set of rules. You are always shooting at a moving target. That's an issue.

If I'm going to sell a Client on SEO, I need to believe in the value of the offering enough that the potential negative (the constantly moving target) is far outweighed by the upside of higher ranking and more traffic. Further, my prospects are going to know about this "issue" long before I ever have the opportunity to engage with them. This means that I need to have honest answers to their questions and a response to the "what do you do when Google rolls out the next update?" question.

These negatives are qualifiers of which you need to be aware because you're going to be on the receiving end of them. As the digital marketer, you're the front line of defense and you need to be able to speak to them and be prepared to mitigate the impact they have on the sales cycle.

This is why you need to believe in what you're selling. The days of snake oil are coming to an end. Yes, there are still a ton of scam artists making money on crummy products that don't do what they say they're going to do. But there's no way to build a business around it, not anymore. There are courses that teach unscrupulous marketers how to maneuver merchant processing disputes to still make a profit when they're selling a product they know will have a high potential for charge backs.

It's getting harder and harder to be dishonest. The easiest thing to do is to stop looking for better ways to hide and just start doing good business. Don't take Clients that have an offering you don't believe in. Don't take Clients that sell something that you wouldn't buy assuming you were in their target demographic. Your reputation is going to very quickly become tethered to the companies that you represent. Even more than that, your ability to be successful is going to be completely dependent on the viability of the offering that you're marketing.

Yes, a good digital marketer can sell a bad product. I've seen it happen. But it usually doesn't last long. That's what the information based economy has done for us. It protects consumers and punishes those that seek to deceive.

The case for ethical business isn't just a lip service conversation any longer. Good business makes good business sense. Honesty and integrity are virtues that now come equipped with magnifying glasses and microscopes. Prospects can look at your business more closely than ever before and without you even knowing about it. So keep the windows clean, the closets tidy and only bring things into the fold that you will be proud of.

Chapter **2**

THE 7 CRITICAL PRINCIPLES OF EFFECTIVE DIGITAL MARKETING

OKAY, ENOUGH OF THE FOUNDATION BUILDING STUFF. LET'S TALK SHOP. There are 7 Critical principles of effective digital marketing:

PARADIGM PRINCIPLES

1. Empathize
2. Give value first, always
3. Learn, apply & innovate

PROCESS PRINCIPLES

1. Use a living plan
2. Use appropriate tools effectively
3. Use human capital effectively
4. Scale: synergize, integrate and automate

Chapter 2

Figure 1 illustrates the construct of these principles in terms of how they relate to each other.

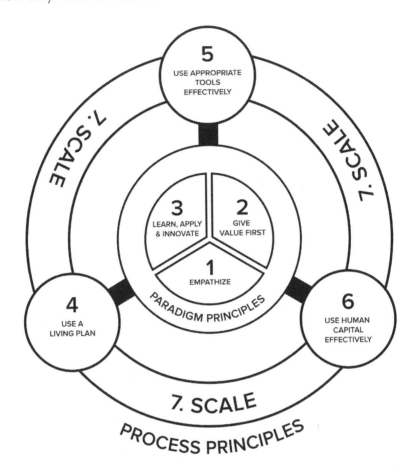

Figure 1. Construct of Principles

The paradigm principles (1 through 3) need to be at the core of all other initiatives. These are the principles that impact and guide your thoughts and decision making as a digital marketer. They are the lens through which you view the digital marketing world and are foundational in importance.

The process principles are the principles that guide our execution. Principles 4, 5 & 6 are all interconnected by the 7th principle: scale. In many cases, you'll find that these principles are interdependent and can't exist without each other.

You will also notice that the principles are articulated as verbs. This is by design and meant to contextualize them in a way that will be most effective to the reader. Where "empathy" is a concept, empathize is an act and habit. You don't carry concepts with you into processes very often but it's extremely easy to apply actions to processes. Learning the principles as verbs instead of nouns (actions instead of concepts) will help to reinforce their proper placement in terms of how, when and where they should be utilized.

In the realm of digital marketing (and in education in general) there is far too much emphasis placed on ethereal, nebulous and conceptual ideas that have very little possibility for practical application. By articulating our principles in a way that verb-alizes (get it?) their action we reinforce and strengthen the subconscious understanding that this is not just something you learn but something you do.

OTHER PRINCIPLES

WHEN I PRESENT THE 7 CRITICAL PRINCIPLES TO OTHER DIGITAL MARKETERS, I am sometimes met with a handful of challenges to the order, construct or even inclusion of what I have identified as the 7 Critical Principles. Sometimes I'm challenged with the reason a certain principle or concept doesn't exist within the 7.

While I'm sure there are areas or situations where it might be appropriate to revise the core 7 principles, I feel very strongly that these represent the foundational and prerequisite principles for effective digital marketing.

In fact, the vast majority of challenges I've met with result in the discovery that the "missing principle" is already housed within one of the larger, overarching principles. Within the paradigm principles, this is especially true for the first and most important principle: empathize.

We will discuss the application of the principle in subsequent sections but, for now, suffice it to say that to empathize acts as a guiding light for nearly all decisions that may impact a customer's digital marketing journey. That's not to say that the principles potentially housed beneath it are less important, only that they are included in the paradigm already being presented.

An additional challenge I have received (and one that annoys me to no end) is the apparent lack of basic and more traditional "life" principles. Principles such as honesty and diligence (just for example) aren't spoken to directly and therefore may appear to be disassociated with the principles I have set forth. While I do contend that many of these base principles are reflected within and throughout this book, I admit that I have not taken the time to speak to them directly. Their apparent absence isn't a reflection upon their importance. In fact, it's the exact opposite.

Principles are natural and governing laws of an organic system. The principles we are discussing here are those that apply specifically and explicitly to the realm of digital marketing. More traditional principles such as truth, justice, temperance, fairness, etc., are equally important and maybe even more so in the realm of most human endeavors. But they are not exclusive to digital marketing.

Further, there are far too many "life principles" to name, describe and then qualify the application of, within the context of digital marketing. So I have chosen to assume that my reader comes equipped with at least a basic understanding of general human decency and does not need a refresher course in the core tenets of not being a horrible person.

If you do find yourself in need of a book to tell you not to lie, cheat, steal, murder or pillage, I recommend The Children's Book of Virtues by William J. Bennett. Otherwise, let's please continue with the precondition that these are assumed and axiomatic foundations of our collective consciousness.

PARADIGM PRINCIPLES OVERVIEW

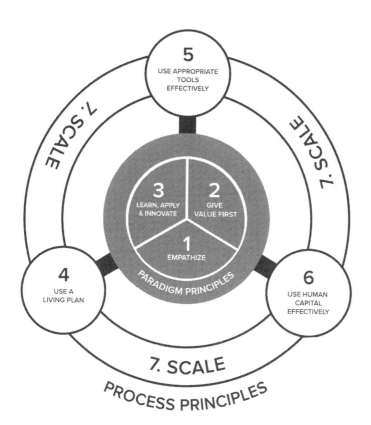

- 5 USE APPROPRIATE TOOLS EFFECTIVELY
- 3 LEARN, APPLY & INNOVATE
- 2 GIVE VALUE FIRST
- 1 EMPATHIZE
- PARADIGM PRINCIPLES
- 4 USE A LIVING PLAN
- 6 USE HUMAN CAPITAL EFFECTIVELY
- 7. SCALE
- PROCESS PRINCIPLES

THE PARADIGMS THROUGH WHICH WE VIEW THE WORLD WILL DICTATE HOW we see it. The truth of your experience isn't an objective understanding—it never has been. Your truth is the story you tell yourself and that story is told through the proxy of your paradigm. The very first thing we need to do in order to cultivate an effective and principle-centered approach to digital marketing is to make sure we adequately define our paradigms. The paradigm principles are the "why." These principles are:

- Empathize
- Be the first (and last) to give value
- Learn, apply & innovate

The paradigm principles are a direct reflection of how we approach the concept of digital marketing from a philosophical perspective. These three principles are the most important because they will set the tone for how the process principles are carried out. While the process principles help us to define the "how"—how we execute, what steps we take, the strategies we use, etc.—the paradigm principles help us to define the "why".

As with all things, the "why" is always of paramount importance. In fact, often, having the "why" will yield the "how" with relative ease. Understanding the core paradigm principles is a prerequisite to being able to use the process principles. Without the foundation of the paradigm principles, the process principles drop off their principle pedestal and plunge down to become nothing more than tactics.

It isn't enough to know what the paradigm principles are – you have to truly commit to living them. Build them into your thought process so that they become second nature. As marketers, we tend to look for patterns and, in so doing, cultivate habits. Your habits will make or break you more than any other single facet of life. So, make sure the habits you form are habits you have chosen and not ones that have grown from negligence or simply by default.

While the process principles cannot exist without the paradigm principles, the paradigm principles carry no level of dependence. They exist with or without the combination of any outside influence. The paradigm principles will have an immense impact on everything you do in the realm of digital marketing. They are truly invaluable.

PRINCIPLE 1
EMPATHIZE

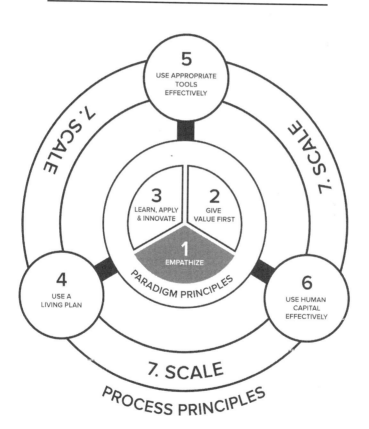

Empathy is the most powerful word in the English language.

- Anonymous

em·pa·thy \ 'em-pə-thē \ *n* : the ability to understand and share the feelings of another

- Webster's Dictionary, 1869

EMPATHY, IN THE CONTEXT OF DIGITAL MARKETING, IS YOUR ABILITY TO PLACE yourself in your prospect's shoes and feel what they are feeling. It speaks to your ability to understand their pain points, what they value and why, what their past experiences might have been, what makes them purchase, what messaging appeals to them and what kind of person they want to do business with.

Empathy is the foundational principle on which all the other principles of digital marketing reside. There is no greater skill a digital marketer may possess and no other principle worthier of our habitual utilization and exercise.

It is my personal experience that your powers of empathy can be honed and expanded. Like any other tool in your mental/emotional arsenal, empathy can be strengthened and sharpened with focused attention.

While empathy as a preconditioned human response usually comes naturally to most people, it isn't quite as ubiquitous an approach in our marketing endeavors. For some reason, when we strap on our business hats, we decide that's an appropriate queue to go stupid in certain realms of thought that would otherwise yield more emotionally intelligent results.

Think back to your own experiences in shopping for products or services. When someone is able to speak to your exact needs, meaning they address your pain points, present the value you're seeking in terms you agree with and outline the process of acquisition in a way that resonates with your personal purchasing procedure, you can't hit "go" fast enough!

There is a stigma to empathy as a concept that we all need to get over very quickly. Empathy as a paradigm has been treated as though it is an infantile concept that should be reserved for kindergarten classrooms and sharing circles. I believe this is because business people, in all their brilliance, have led themselves to believe that professionalism in business is the absence of certain human preconditions. The view is that things like emotions and feelings should be left out of board room conversations.

Maybe there's merit to the sterilization of the human condition within boardroom settings. I wouldn't know, I'm not a business consultant or efficiency expert, I'm a digital marketer. However, I can tell you that, in the realm of digital marketing, feelings matter. It's what makes people buy.

People buy because they believe they are going to **feel** something. It might be fulfillment, ease, stress relief, excitement, whatever, but they aren't purchasing a product or a service, they are purchasing a feeling. Purchasing decisions are not logical and they never will be. They are psychological and they're driven by emotional responses.

BUILDING AN AVATAR

YOUR AVATAR IS A REPRESENTATION OF YOUR IDEAL CUSTOMER (OR YOUR Client's ideal customer). In many cases, you may have more than one Avatar. An Avatar is not a "target demographic" which is a target group. An Avatar is a single, idealized individual. Think of Avatar building as building a person. You are going to identify and define the inner workings of who this person really is and not just from a professional standpoint either.

This is a process that gets a whole lot of lip service and very little real attention as soon as the digital rubber meets the marketing road. I think people tend to view this step as too academic. They don't ask the question because they feel they already know the answers. However, the answers are never as obvious as they may seem.

This becomes more and more apparent as you begin asking different people associated with the campaign the same questions. You'll see very quickly that, if you haven't worked to define an Avatar, you are often targeting very different people, even within your own organization.

If empathy is the most important principle in digital marketing, then knowing who it is you are meant to empathize with is the most important step. That's what building your Avatar is and it should not be skipped. This is especially true for digital marketers who are working on other people's campaigns. When you take on a new Client this is the very first piece of real work you should be doing.

Here are some examples of Avatar building questions:

- What does their average day look like?
- How do they spend their free time?
- What are their goals?
- What are their values?
- What are their challenges?
- What are their pain points?
- Where do they go for information?
- What sources of media do they trust?
- What influencers do they listen to?
- When do they typically engage with content?
  o ...and through what medium?
- What does their peer group look like?
- What associations are they a part of?
- How educated are they?
- What are their worries and concerns?
- What responsibilities do they have?
- What completely turns them off?

This isn't a comprehensive list of questions. It's more of a guideline as to the types of questions you should be asking yourself when building your Avatar.

As you can see, your Avatar isn't your "target demographic." Instead of speaking to your potential prospects as a group (the way "target demographic" does) you are going to speak to them as an individual. In some cases, you may need to create multiple Avatars.

In the vast majority of cases you're going to find that certain levels of specificity are required to begin to realize the value that comes in defining your Avatar. Not all the questions I have posed above are going to be relevant or applicable. However, there are a few channels of thought that, if you follow them through to completion, will yield amazing results in your marketing efforts.

To give you an example, one of the verticals that we focus on often is medical marketing. My target demographic may be defined as: owners and managing physicians of private medical practices with an emphasis on pain management. We have built two Avatars for this vertical. Our experience in this market has taught us that there are two primary Avatars (based upon our previous customers). I've included an abridged version of our Avatar below:

Dr. Mike

- Male
- Early 50s
- Married
- Two adult children
- Behaviors:
  - Interested in ultimately transitioning out of the practice. This can be accomplished through a sale or by bringing on a junior partner. For this reason, Dr. Mike is very focused on stable and long-term marketing campaigns so he can feel comfortable stepping away.
  - Often delegates heavily to a junior partner or office manager. In some instances, this person can be the initial contact for digital marketing engagement.
- Primary pain points:
  - Dr. Mike doesn't always understand the nuances of digital marketing. He doesn't have the same level of comfort with it as do his younger contemporaries. He's intelligent and well educated but is unwilling to abdicate the final decision to a vendor. He needs concepts explained clearly and succinctly in order for him to get to a decision point.
  - Dr. Mike has very limited time. Touch points should be limited and all reporting should be truncated to the absolute essentials. Attempt to work as often as possible through the Office Manager.
- Values:
  - Dr. Mike is interested in campaign initiatives that can be tied directly to revenue.
  - Dr. Mike values efficiency. Be respectful of his time and react quickly to requests or suggestions.
- Sources of information:

- o Industry publications and trade journals.
- o [We have a detailed list of these compiled that includes over 50 digital and analog publications]

Dr. Jenny

- Female
- Early 30s
- Single
- No children
- Behaviors:
  - o Dr. Jenny offers a broad range of services and is willing to experiment with what works in terms of how she presents herself.
  - o Dr. Jenny is very involved in the building of her practice and tends to be extremely hands on.
- Primary pain points:
  - o Dr. Jenny is working with a limited budget but has extremely big ideas. She "gets it" when it comes to digital marketing and wants to do everything all at once but often can't afford the big bite approach.
  - o Dr. Jenny is starting from zero and needs to build up her Client base, email list and visibility.
- Values:
  - o Dr. Jenny values visibility and reach. She understands the importance of building a large following and aggregating a list of subscribers.
  - o Dr. Jenny wants to be very cutting edge. She is brand and image conscious and likes being involved in the digital marketing campaign creation process.
- Sources of information:
  - o Industry publications and trade journals.
  - o Facebook and LinkedIn.

Do you see how different each of these Avatars is? They're in the exact same "target demographic" and yet, as people, they would respond to completely different messaging. Further, do you see the value in beginning to define them as individuals? This definition is what places us in the position to be able to begin our empathic process.

Your Avatar is a representation of what you (or your Client) know about the people that they serve. It's okay to include anecdotal evidence and information that isn't entirely data driven. It's especially "okay" because this information doesn't exist anywhere else. You're making educated guesses and assumptions based upon what you know about an existing user group. In fact, part of your value as a marketer is going to be how good you get at doing so.

This plays indirectly with a concept we will talk about later: making intuitive decisions and then using data for adjustments. There might not be any data available on what types of publications your Avatar reads or when they check their email. It's okay for you to play the "correlation *is* causation" game just as long as you understand the purpose of the exercise and the need to validate, test and revisit your assumptions later.

You should never be done building your Avatar. As your marketing campaigns expand, you should continuously be adding, deleting and editing your definition to get closer to a core focus as to whom you are marketing. In some cases, you may end up adding a new Avatar or splitting an existing one into two if you define a large enough segment.

The focus of the Avatar building process needs to be understanding who you are speaking to. This understanding will tie directly into your ability to adequately empathize with this person. Reflect on it often and make sure that you're approaching your Avatar from a vantage point of empathy and not manipulation.

When we begin an academic process like Avatar creation, it's relatively easy to get caught in the trap of "how do I get this person to do [x]" or "how do I trick/convince/coerce them to…whatever." Avatar creation isn't about identifying weaknesses or psychological back doors. It's about building an understanding of your prospect that enables you to think and feel the way they may think and feel.

AVATARS AND EMPATHY

THE HIGHER IN THE SALES FUNNEL YOU ARE ABLE TO CAPTURE A POTENTIAL prospect, the less expensive they'll be. Said another way, your cost per acquisition will rise as the user's position in the sales funnel falls. For example, someone who goes to Google and searches for "best website design company in Phoenix, Arizona" is already close to a buying decision and, therefore, the cost per acquisition on this customer is going to be competitive.

This is true regardless of your approach. If you attempt to organically optimize the key phrase or simply bid on the click, the space is competitive and so the time, effort, energy and potential spend are going to be priced accordingly. Your ability to capture that prospect's attention is also going to be diluted by the fact that your competition is going to be vying for their attention as well. This means that the noise to which the prospect is subjected will make differentiating yourself more difficult.

However, once you've learned more about your target Avatar, you'll be equipped to find them earlier in the funnel. Using the website example above, we determined that the vast majority of our new website customers were website rebuilds. Because our price point is higher than the first-time website purchaser may believe s/he needs, we typically fare better after a prospect has had the opportunity to see what types of tradeoffs come with a cheap website.

Using that knowledge, we can build an understanding of what would catalyze a prospect's need for a website rebuild. Three of the primary pain points we established when we defined our Avatar were things like a recent hack, the inability to update content and the lack of a responsive design (which used to be a more prevalent issue than it is now). This gives us the opportunity to build content, bid on or optimize key phrases and market to potential prospects earlier in the sales funnel.

Before the prospect is searching for "best website design company in Phoenix, Arizona" s/he is going to be searching for things like "how to fix a website that has been hacked" or "how to make my website responsive." We're now able to capture that prospect prior to their transitioning to a purchase decision because we have "found" them earlier in the sales funnel. This requires that we employ empathy to determine how to engage them appropriately according to their specific needs.

This not only means that they'll be less expensive as a lead (since their search terms are far less competitive) it also means that we'll be given the opportunity to market in a silo. Marketing in a silo means you're no longer marketing against other providers, you're now marketing as though you're the only solution. Now you're simply qualifying their needs against the solutions you have available.

There's virtually no limit to how high you can go in attempting to capture prospects earlier in their sales journey. Remember, the earlier you capture them the less expensive they'll be as leads but the longer it'll take to nurture them into qualified prospects. If you're looking to attract new home buyers, instead of bidding on key phrases like "buy a house in [wherever]" (which is close to the bottom of the sales funnel) you might start looking for prospects that have shown interest in pre-qualification.

That would be one step earlier in the sales funnel. However, after defining your Avatar, you may realize that most of your new home buyers are newly married couples. If that's true, then you can begin targeting newlyweds or recently engaged couples through social channels that allow that level of segmentation. If your Avatar tends to be families with small children that are up-sizing their homes to accommodate their new additions, you can target couples that are showing interest in having babies.

The way you target these interests and the way you position yourself as a thought leader are things for which you'll need to find and build a strategy. Some interests or user activity are more difficult to segment than others. Facebook has the ability to target new parents by checking a box but if you're attempting to target expectant parents, you might need to get more creative. What content networks would expectant parents be engaging with? What online properties would they visit? What email lists would they subscribe to? You can place your message in their line of sight, you just need to determine what that is.

Sometimes as you travel higher in the sales funnel you dilute the possibility that a potential prospect would ever become a lead at all. For example, assume you're targeting college students who are searching for student loan services. This is an extremely competitive space. Moving higher in the awareness funnel would find you targeting students applying to college. Moving higher still would find you targeting high school students who are going to be graduating soon.

This positioning in the funnel will yield a less expensive lead from a CPA (cost per acquisition) standpoint but you'll also have a diluted quality of prospect since not every high school graduate is going to apply to college (just as not every newlywed couple is going to buy a house and not every business with a recently hacked website is going to opt for a complete rebuild). The idea would be that the decreased cost per acquisition in generating leads higher in the funnel would justify the dilution in lead quality. If you ever find that this isn't the case, then you might have traveled too high in the sales funnel and need to bring your focus further down.

Sometimes capturing users prior to their being qualified prospects isn't possible. In other cases, it isn't profitable. However, the sooner you are able to attract the attention of a potential prospect, the sooner you'll begin to establish yourself as a thought leader and build a value-based relationship with that person. The longer you're able to engage that prospect the more likely it is that they become a qualified lead and, ideally, a new customer.

B2B, B2C, B2P & P2P

EMPATHY IS A FEELING. DEMOGRAPHICS DON'T FEEL. FOCUS GROUPS DON'T feel. People feel. In order to fully buy into the concept of empathy as a foundational focus for digital marketing, we need to first understand something of massive importance: there is no such thing as B2B (business to business) or B2C (business to consumer) marketing.

That line in the sand was drawn a million years ago when analog marketing was still a thing. It is an absurd assumption made by people who don't understand the way markets are to be engaged in the digital realm. It's a carry-over concept from the days of traditional media and it needs to be shot in the face and buried in the backyard without a funeral.

Digital marketing is B2P, business to person. Do you speak to someone differently when they're making a business purchase instead of a personal purchase? Sure. The same way you speak differently so someone who is purchasing personal hygiene products compared to someone who is purchasing food products, or dog toys, or rocket fuel. But you still speak to them like they're people... because they are.

Part of the reason that so many B2B companies continue to subscribe to the idea that digital marketing doesn't work (or is less effective) is because of the standard B2B approach they are taking to digital marketing. It's a self-fulfilling prophecy. The sterile, hands off, "just the facts" approach that B2B companies make in their digital marketing efforts is a recipe for disaster. You can't empathize with a business any more than you can empathize with a "consumer group".

You don't sell to a company—you sell to a person. You need to know your target buyer on a personal level, not just a company level. You might be targeting companies that manufacture military vehicles but that's not your Avatar. Your Avatar would be the engineer, project manager, or buyer assigned to making that purchasing decision.

In some cases, you'll have multiple Avatars. In a few rare cases I have seen what we called "stacked" Avatars; situations where there are always two decision makers out of necessity for the process. One of our Clients manufactured equipment for medical procedures; the buyer was almost always a two-person team: the head of major medical and the hospital administrator. The Doctor was there to ensure the product suited their medical requirements and the administrator was there to make sure the product met their business requirements. We built marketing that spoke to both.

Now, please don't misunderstand what I'm saying. When you're building your Avatar, the B2B/B2C distinction will help define the person you're targeting, but it's still a person that you're speaking to. That's the important distinction I'm trying to make. Empathy starts with a person. The definition of who that person is and what demographic group they belong to is important but it's secondary to who they are and how they feel.

As we have said, digital marketing is relationship building. You don't build relationships with demographics or companies, you build them with people. What's interesting is that this concept works in both directions. People are far more likely to buy from a person than a company. This is the P2P approach to digital marketing. In fact, the ability to catalyze a relationship developed from empathic reciprocity is often only possible in a person to person (P2P) environment.

I realize that P2P is not always possible. However, if you ever have the option or opportunity to brand yourself (or your salespeople) in a way that personalizes your marketing message then you absolutely should. You can build a dual relationship with your prospects. The first relationship is with your business (your brand) and the second relationship is with your point of contact. Each stands only to strengthen the other as long as they remain positive.

In fact, the more personal you are willing to get with your prospects the faster your relationship will grow and the stronger it will be. You have probably seen this a dozen or more times as of late, and you may not have even noticed it. Digital marketers weave their personal experiences into the narrative of their marketing to make a connection with their prospects.

It is so much easier for us to purchase from people that truly know what we've gone through, meaning people that can *empathize* with our situation. If I'm overweight, I would rather purchase a fitness and nutrition program from someone who has been overweight and overcame it than someone who has been fit all their lives. How could that second person understand the struggles I have faced?

Again, this is just as easily applied to B2B markets. As digital marketers, we almost exclusively service other businesses. Getting personal about learning and executing on digital marketing should be extremely easy for us! It's not about reflecting on the exact experience that they're having as much as it is explaining how and why you understand what they're going through.

WHO ARE YOU SERVING?

AN EXCELLENT BAROMETER YOU CAN USE IF YOU'RE INTERESTED IN DETERmining whether or not you're operating from a place of empathy, is to ask yourself, "Who am I serving?" If Digital Marketing is relationship building, the strongest relationships are built through service to one another. The person you are serving is the person you are attempting to build a relationship with.

The answer isn't always as clear as you might think. In many cases, you'll find that you are actually serving "The Client," meaning the person who is paying you to conduct digital marketing services on their behalf. While this may make sense from the outside looking in, it's short-sighted and will result in a less effective digital marketing campaign. Allow me the luxury of a small piece of cyclical thought: the best way to serve The Client is to make sure the person your digital marketing campaigns are serving is your Client's Prospect.

In some cases, you'll find that the person you're serving is internal. The campaign is built in a way that will drive the most amount of a certain type of lead because that's what your sales Director or CEO has asked for. You could be attempting to serve yourself by building campaigns that play to your own vanity or sense of "the way it should be." The point is that, if you're operating from a place of empathy, you want to make sure that the empathy is directed at the right person!

All too often we market according to our own needs instead of the needs of the end user. An example of this that quite a few digital marketers are guilty of, is marketing to the data. What I mean by that is marketing in a way that allows you the greatest ability to report positive data to your Clients. Instead of taking a longer-term approach that will ultimately serve a potential prospect better, the campaign is built in such a way that will show the greatest amount of success in the shortest period of time.

The concept of marketing to the data is a perfect example of the difference between personality ethic and character ethic. A great example I have often seen is the free give away or social contest. In an attempt to help build a social following, I have seen agencies offer giveaways, freebies and the opportunity to win really awesome prizes just for following a brand online. The most common prize for quite a few years was an iPad. "We're giving away 1 iPad every day! Like our page for a chance to win."

And these campaigns worked! They brought massive amounts of traffic to their target pages and made the marketers in charge look like rock stars. The issue with this approach is that they weren't approaching their campaigns with the proper sense of empathy. Who wants to win an iPad? Everyone! So who did they get to like their page? Everyone! This did nothing but dilute their reach and force them into a position where their entire list was made up of a completely un-targeted and unsegmented group of disgruntled prospects who (statistically speaking) did not win the iPad.

This marketing to the data might have purchased some awesome reports but it didn't produce any real value. A far more effective campaign would have been to give something away that pertained directly to the company's core offer. A courier service we worked with offered a free month of deliveries. They didn't get anywhere near the traffic that a free iPad would've got them but they received ravenous attention from every single company we were able to put them in front of *that actually used courier services.* That giveaway was an amazing value only if a prospect was actually in their demographic.

Empathy isn't just meant to be the ultimate qualifier. It's also meant to be utilized as a strategic disqualifier. Try to find messaging, offers and strategies that speak specifically to your Avatar and, whenever possible, only your Avatar.

THE OLD SALES FUNNEL VS. THE NEW SALES FUNNEL

THE SALES FUNNEL IS THE PROCESS THROUGH WHICH A CUSTOMER TRAVELS when purchasing products or services. Keep in mind that the stages of the sales funnel are a topic of constant contention and I am not here to propose one over another. The funnel I'm putting forth I'm using for the sake of ease as it is the one I have known to be the most traditional.

The sales funnel (see Figure 2) is an empathic tool that we use in order to try and contextualize a prospect's purchasing readiness. Empathy lives at the core of the sales funnel as a concept and is the single most important element in interpreting a prospect's placement within any funnel. Digital marketing has completely altered the way the sales funnel functions. Here's an image of a traditional sales funnel:

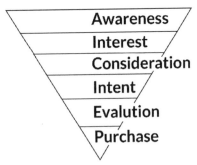

Figure 2. Traditional Sales Funnel

What's interesting to note is that, in the past, marketing has traditionally only been involved in the first three phases of the sales funnel. Awareness and interest rested very firmly in marketing's camp and somewhere in the middle of consideration the prospect would be introduced to a salesperson and the sales department would assume responsibility for the rest of the funnel. The entire rest of the sales funnel became a manual and "in-person" process.

You already know that's no longer the case. Not only is digital marketing very firmly involved (and as often, completely responsible for) the entire sales funnel, the sales funnel has actually been expanded. Here's a look at the new sales funnel (Figure 3):

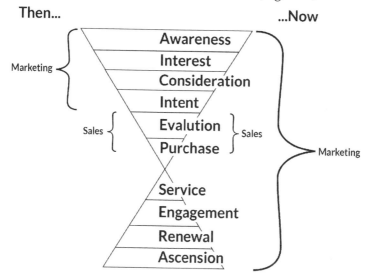

Figure 3. New Sales Funnel

Because digital marketing is relationship building it has become imperative that the practice of digital marketing be carried through the sales funnel into post purchase sequences and processes. This manifests itself in several ways. The customer relationship needs to continue to be nurtured which is the prime directive of digital marketing. We've all read the statistics on how much costlier it is to earn a new customer than to keep an existing one.

Ideally, digital marketing will have a direct impact on the fulfillment process as well. Customer training and onboarding, aggregating reviews and testimonials, asking for referrals, satisfaction surveys, retention campaigns, and ascension campaigns are all examples of digital marketing practices being placed in the post-purchase sequence.

As digital marketers, we need to bring empathy into the post purchase equation. This starts with placing ourselves in our new customer's shoes and asking empathic questions.

- What problems might a new customer encounter immediately after making a purchase?
- What types of training or support would help a new customer?
- What are the primary pain points a new customer experiences with our offering?
- How can we improve the new customer experience post-purchase?
- What additional products or services will a new customer be interested in after their purchase?
- What new products or services would help amplify the value of their new purchase?

Making sure that the digital marketing paradigm includes the entire sales funnel is imperative to continuing the relationship building process. This means empathizing with our new customers just as much as we empathize with potential prospects. Work to bring value in excess and without being asked for it. This means empathizing with your new customers and working to improve their experience.

FIND THE SALES FUNNEL

I BELIEVE THE ABSOLUTE BEST APPROACH TO BUILDING A SALES FUNNEL IS attempting to determine and replicate the path that prospects are already taking to a purchase decision. What we as marketers need to understand is that people are going to travel through a sales funnel with or without us. The sales funnel isn't something that we created, it's simply the logical sequence a person takes when they're on a buying journey.

A prospect who is shopping for a new computer is going to travel through a type of sales funnel completely on their own and without prompting. The awareness of their need will lead to interest in the product and that interest will result in research which catalyzes consideration. As they consider their options they develop intent, the intention to purchase results in detailed evaluation and, ultimately, their evaluation results in a purchase. The sales funnel is completely organic in structure and nothing more than a visual representation of what people already do when they shop.

While the funnel that you build can and absolutely should influence certain factors in their journey, you are going to be far better off if you try to replicate the existing, logical sales funnel than if you attempt to build it to suit your own purposes. For example, you can catalyze awareness (the commonly accepted first stage to any sales funnel) but the concepts and types of information that come coupled with awareness are things you shouldn't attempt to change without at least having a value-added purpose.

When you're building your marketing campaigns, spend some time looking at consumer purchasing behavior and attempting to identify the logical sales funnel that is already in existence. For example, how does awareness usually come about if not catalyzed by a marketer? Using the example of a prospect shopping for a computer, you may find that most new computer purchases are the result of a virus or the crash of an old computer. Assuming that's the case, you can now speak to those specific pain points as you work to attract prospects to your funnel and generate interest.

When a prospect is interested, what information is required for them to seriously consider the product and move into intent? A huge sticking point with digital marketers is whether or not to make pricing available online. This is an argument that circles itself many times and it obviously depends heavily on the product or service. However, if the logical sales funnel that's already been established by the industry is such that user intent can't or won't be established without pricing then you are going to block your own chances of moving a prospect down your funnel if you choose to be non-compliant with that standard.

The information that a user will want to know about an offering, their pain points, the value propositions in which they are most interested, the purchase cycle and terms of purchase, are typically already established norms within most industries. Again, you're absolutely allowed to change or influence them as long as you have a value-added purpose. However, attempting to subvert, skip or mask them is going to put you at odds with a logical and organic system and, ultimately, will result in a failed funnel.

One example I can provide of subverting the existing funnel with a value-added purpose is in custom Salesforce integration. I was shopping on behalf of a Client and found a service provider that refused to list their hourly rate on their site. Salesforce providers typically make their rates available so this was definitely a break from the established norm. However, their stated value proposition was that they didn't charge by the hour at all. Instead, they would bid a project by the job, submit a flat fee proposal and, regardless of how long the work took, the Client would only have to pay the proposed fee.

The value proposition here is compelling, especially because the work required isn't always easy to anticipate or scope. They were offering to assume the financial risk of any potential scope creep and, in so doing, were able to modify the sales funnel. I was interested enough in their offer to request a custom quote just to see what their milestone-based pricing structure would look like.

There are always going to be opportunities for you to improve on the sales funnel that already exists within the industry to which you're marketing. The important consideration you need to make as a marketer is what the established sales funnel looks like and what types of expectations your prospects are going to have coming into it.

All too often we look at the sales funnel as a tool that serves our purposes in qualifying a prospect and driving a purchase. Instead, we need to look at the sales funnel as a tool we've built to help a prospect make a purchasing decision by fulfilling their needs and requirements. And, as with most things, you're allowed to break the rules but only after you know what they are. The existing sales funnel is almost always in place because it's simply the most logical sequence to a correct purchase decision. Unless you have an improvement to it, trying to change it purely for your own benefit will only result in a broken funnel.

UTILIZING EMPATHY

As we have already discussed, there is a very simple formula for how effective digital marketing is accomplished:

Digital Marketing = Relationship Building = Content + Context

Keep in mind, digital marketing is still relationship building. We're not changing our definition—we're defining the "how" in terms of execution. The internet is a conduit for content dissemination. Everything you engage with online, every word, sound, video and image is considered content.

Digital marketing is the act of creating valuable content, content that is meant to catalyze a specific action, and then strategically contextualizing that content according to your Avatar in order to build a value-driven relationship. The sales funnel is a visual articulation of this strategic contextualization of content as a complete process. Each stage in the funnel is a different piece of content with a different context applied to it.

The importance of the content should be axiomatic and is something I believe we can all agree on. However, the importance of the context is a little more difficult to define and agree on because it's extremely elusive as a concept. By empathizing with our Avatar, we can work to understand what context and timing is most important for a piece of content. As you work to empathize with your Avatar, there is a collection of important questions you can ask yourself.

Where am I approaching my Avatar? When applied to the question of context, the "where" defines the online network or medium through which your prospect will be engaging with your content. "Where" should have a massive impact on how the content is prepared and what types of content you use. An email should take a wildly different form than a blog or press release. A Facebook ad is a much different approach than a Google AdWords ad.

Am I a destination or a distraction? For example, if someone searches for "Best PPC company" and my ad appears for that search, I am a potential destination. The ad is the content and the search result is the context. On the other hand, if someone is scrolling through their Facebook feed and they see my sponsored post advertising my PPC services, I am a distraction. The intention of their current experience wasn't to engage with me or my brand.

One isn't necessarily better than the other. However, the change in context requires a change in approach. This is the power of empathy in terms of context. You can be discussing the exact same Avatar and the exact same offering and yet, given a different context, your entire approach may need to change. If you're a destination, you can speak directly to your value proposition with the expectation of engagement. If you're a distraction, you're more likely going to deliver extremely valuable content in an effort to first engage and then convert your prospect.

Neither approach is better or worse, but it is very important to understand which approach applies to your specific purpose so you can properly contextualize your content. When you're a destination, you have the luxury of speaking directly to value. When you're a distraction, you need to be more engaging and be comfortable with a longer, nurtured approach.

How does my Avatar expect to be approached? There are rules of engagement, social contracts, community understandings and (sometimes) terms of services that need to be met with when you are contextualizing content. If you have any experience in using forums as a marketing channel you know how quickly and easily a group or community can turn on a potential marketer. Joining a forum for the sole purpose of attempting to market a product is a massive breach of etiquette and sure to get you permanently banned.

However, if you join a forum and work to actively and consistently provide value and build relationships with other forum members, you will never find more willing participants in soft launches, product reviews and even potential affiliates. These communities are absolute gold mines as long as they are approached with respect and engaged with on their own terms. This is true of every possible marketing medium.

Users begin to develop certain expectations as to how a medium is meant to be used. When you abuse or misalign yourself with those expectations you are doing a poor job of properly contextualizing your content. A great example of this is LinkedIn in-mail. This is a phenomenal tool that, when utilized well, can give you direct access to a high value decision maker's inbox. I have used this more times than I can count to put a targeted and specific offer in front of a potential prospect that I wouldn't otherwise ever have had access to.

The expectation, however, is that your offer truly be something of immense value to the recipient. This is especially true when you're approaching prospects that might otherwise be out of reach. A great example I have seen of this being done successfully comes from someone who has become a long-time vendor of mine. He provides whiteboard explainer videos and wanted to build his portfolio of work, increase his exposure and elevate his brand by cultivating a recognizable Client list.

He sent me a LinkedIn in-mail message offering me a completely free 3-minute explainer video on any topic of my choosing. The video was mine to keep without any cost or obligation. If, at the end of the process, I was happy with the end result he provided a guest blog for potential inclusion in our company blog. The blog (which he shared in the message) was very well written and would be of immense value to my readers. The only self-serving element was a very soft reference to his services at the end of the blog.

Of course, I said yes! His content (the message with his offer) matched my contextual expectations of a cold message from LinkedIn. Compare this to the countless number of messages I receive asking me for my time to listen to some sales pitch and you can immediately see how and why he was successful.

What voice or tone would appeal to my Avatar and why? Every Avatar is going to expect to be engaged with differently. If you're marketing to a group of engineers, you will speak to them differently than a group of college athletes. The voice you utilize when constructing your content can also be impacted by the context within which that content will ultimately reside. For example, the same exact Avatar will be far more forgiving of colloquial language when it's on a social media channel than they will when it's in an email.

Each content conduit will have its own unique voice. It's your job to understand how that conduit is used and apply that expectation to your content according to your Avatar. Hopefully, you're starting to see the layers of interdependent contextual considerations that are involved in creating content. A video on YouTube is going to be wildly different than a video on Snapchat. They are two completely different networks and they have two completely different sets of expectations from their user base. This is true even if we're talking about the same users!

What basic understanding of my topic does my Avatar have and/ or what lack needs to be addressed? Your Avatar's understanding of your brand, product, service, competition and industry is a powerful piece of the contextual definition you can use to help amplify the value of your content. Often, this is something you can assume or qualify based upon the types of content you're using and where you're placing that content.

For example, if I create a piece of content called: "The Beginner's Guide to PPC Landing Pages," I can safely assume that anyone who engages with that content is going to be relatively new to the concept of creating landing pages specifically for paid advertising campaigns. The content yields intrinsic context in terms of who the user is and where they are in the sales funnel.

With what baggage or history might my Avatar be approaching my content? Your target Avatar's history is an extremely important context to apply to any piece of content you plan on using to catalyze them to action. A very specific example I can provide comes from my experience with the dental industry. I have had many dental Clients over the years—it has proven to be one of our strongest and most consistent verticals.

What's interesting about dentists as an Avatar, is that every single dentist I have ever encountered has a distinctly negative opinion of online marketing. This is even true for brand new dentists who just graduated! Even though they have yet to run a practice, they have been indoctrinated by their peers and mentors to believe that digital marketing is an industry full of charlatans and very difficult to succeed in.

This is invaluable context for me to have. In fact, it works to help me define what types of content I use and how I position that content for engagement. When you're approaching an Avatar that has been burned by your industry, the worst thing you can do is ignore their preconceived, negative neuro-associations.

What misconceptions or assumptions will my Avatar possibly be making? You will often find consistency and common denominators in terms of how a certain type of Avatar perceives your service. This is similar to the issue we discussed above with the dentists but can relate to far more than a negative perception or bad experience.

For example, I have noticed a similar consistency in business consultants. We've been engaged by a handful of business consultants over the years and, to stereotype, they tend to have unreasonable expectations as to how well digital marketing can perform. I think this is because there's a large industry built around selling people into business consultation as a type of franchised business.

Tenured business professionals, often retired, are easy targets for these types of "opportunities" and are usually required a certain level of financial buy in as their down payment. During their training, they are educated as to how to find new Clients and digital marketing tends to be an extremely central part of that education. It's in the franchise owner's best interest to make their new students optimistic about the possibilities of their new business. For this reason, digital marketing tends to be oversold as a fast, cheap and easy way to open the floodgates of new Clients.

I love to work with business consultants! They tend not to be very large Clients for us, as even the most successful consultants just don't need an extremely robust marketing campaign to generate enough business to keep them busy. However, when they are successful they are the absolute best referral source I could possibly have. There's no better proof of concept than the fact that my company successfully markets the consultant that a person has trusted to improve their business.

These are a few examples of questions you can ask yourself as you attempt to empathize with your Avatar's contextual placement within the sales funnel. Obviously, this is by no means a comprehensive list. I just want to give you some insight into the practical application of empathy as an approach, especially as it relates to defining context.

IMPORTANCE OF NARRATIVE

THE NARRATIVE IS ONE OF THE OLDEST TRADITIONS IN HUMAN HISTORY. There isn't a culture on the planet that doesn't count narrative custom among its most important cornerstones. Almost all our pastimes, sporting events, music, movies, theatre, television and reading, are deeply rooted in this narrative tradition. Every single major religion is built upon and communicated with the use of narrative. When we empathize with our Avatar, narrative becomes an extremely valuable tool to begin articulating the results our empathic undertakings yield.

People tend to think in a narrative format. It's the reason the narrative is among the most effective teaching tools. Narrative approaches help to increase retention and understanding by putting the person who is interacting with the narrative in a position of active engagement. The interesting thing about the narrative as a format is it brings about empathic reciprocity—meaning your Avatar will begin to empathize with you and your story through the power of the narrative.

The viewer is an integral part of every story because his or her perception gives life to the narrative. This responsibility places people in a position to want to commit to narratives to give life to the story. That's not to say that people won't abandon narratives if they no longer serve their purposes, just that they are more likely to commit to a narrative than to a simple collection of data or facts. Your ability to empathize with your Avatar places you in a position to get them to begin to empathize with your narrative.

What I'm saying is this: when you use the narrative as a marketing tool, your prospects are predisposed to follow it more than any other type or construct of content. You are working with, and calling upon, thousands of years of tradition, massive historical context and (more than likely) immense amounts of neuro-association. People want to hear stories and they want to see them through to the end.

The sales funnel can be a narrative. If you construct your sales funnel well and you truly empathize with your prospect, your sales funnel can tell a complete story that results in your prospect becoming a Client and your Client becoming an advocate.

Here's the interesting thing about narrative as a concept: it's built on empathy. As a species, our obsession with narratives comes from our need to empathize. The narrative is a tool used to catalyze empathy in a way that allows the viewer to feel emotions, think thoughts and experience situations they would otherwise not be able to do.

The entire point of the narrative is to create a safe and approachable context for the application and (sometimes) exploitation of our empathic capabilities. Think about every commercial that has ever made you cry or every song that has ever made you sing until you lost your voice. Think about the books you love and the movies you revisit over and over and over again. The narratives that impact us most are the ones that trigger the most amount of empathy. When we see ourselves in the subject matter, when we identify to a point of taking ownership in the outcome, that's when we are empathizing most.

You have the unique opportunity as a marketer to use this grand tradition in a way that benefits you and your prospect. If you can build an effective narrative, and use that narrative to help educate and inform your Avatar, you'll find yourself with a well-oiled lead machine. The interesting thing about empathy as a principle is that it doesn't just apply to the approach you need to take with your prospects. It can also apply to the emotion you attempt to elicit from you prospect through your content.

NARRATIVE CONTINUITY

ONE OF THE MOST IMPORTANT FACETS OF A NARRATIVE IS MAINTAINING continuity. There's nothing that takes someone out of a story faster than a break in continuity. In practical terms, this means making sure there's a logical sequence of transition between the phases in your sales funnel. You also want the same continuity reflected on a smaller scale when transitioning between pieces of content through a call to action sequence.

Empathy is a paramount facet of continuity because it requires you to think about what someone expects to come next. One of the best examples I can provide is something you probably encounter a hundred times a day or more: email. There's nothing more frustrating than an email that doesn't maintain continuity throughout the email narrative. A single-subject email is typically composed of three parts: subject line, email copy with targeted CTA and the click through destination.

In order to maintain continuity with the presented narrative, each of these three parts would need to align with each other to form a cohesive narrative. The subject line would need to provide a very clear indicator as to what the email is about. If a prospect opens an email the presumption is that whatever the subject line stated was interesting enough to garner his/her attention. To that end, the email copy must speak directly to the content offered in the subject line. If there is a click through destination (like a blog, article, video or press release), that new destination must establish the next step in the narrative.

It's frustrating when you think an email subject line to be of interest and then open that email to find that the content of the email has little or nothing to do with the subject line. This is why I'm not a fan of clickbait email subjects. There's nothing wrong with being creative, but do so in a way that's still descriptive as to what you're offering. Going back to the personality ethic vs character ethic discussion: the personality ethic asks "how do I increase my open rate?" while the character ethic asks "what emails do my prospects want to open?"

Empathy stands at the center of the continuity discussion because it requires that you attempt to understand what your prospect would expect to see with each new step and phase of engagement. You need to place yourself in the prospect's shoes and then make logical assumptions as to what expectations you will trigger with each new step. In the confines of "pull" marketing any catalytic content, which we typically refer to as a call to action, is just a promise of future delivery. If you open *this* email I promise to give you content on *this* subject.

Another great example of the need to maintain continuity is in paid advertising. Have you ever found a pay-per-click ad interesting and then clicked on the ad only to end up on a landing page that doesn't reflect the same offer the ad spoke to? The trust between you and the brand is immediately shattered and you feel victim to a poor bait and switch tactic. This is the worst way to begin a relationship and introduce people to your brand.

Paid advertising needs to maintain continuity throughout the entire buying narrative all the way to and through a completed conversion. The ad you craft should speak to a specific offering. The landing page that results should maintain continuity and continue to speak to the same offering with additional information.

The call to action on the landing page (the button, form, chat box, phone number, etc.) should also speak to the offering. Instead of a simple "buy now" try a more descriptive "Yes! I want my FREE, no-obligation SEO evaluation." The thank you page they land on after completion should recognize exactly what it is they opted in for and the follow up email you send should do the same as well as articulate what they can expect next.

Maintaining continuity throughout the conversion process will build trust with your prospect by constantly and consistently delivering on the small promises you make with each stage of conversion. This continuity helps to build a narrative in the buying process and gives your prospect a greater sense of ease. You remove any room for confusion as to exactly what you have been offering and what they should expect to get.

The final step in maintaining continuity is making sure to deliver on exactly what you have promised. If I promise you an SEO evaluation within 24 hours completely free of cost or obligation, I need to deliver on that promise. The narrative isn't complete until you have the evaluation in hand. Until the narrative is complete you're not going to trust the story I tell you. Fulfillment is as much a part of digital marketing as any other stage in the sales cycle.

This goes back to what we discussed earlier about the expansion of the sales funnel. In the past, the marketing team would have absolutely nothing to do with the fulfillment stage of any product or service. If you bought a chair from a catalog or long distance from a telemarketer at no point did the marketing team get involved in actually fulfilling your offer. They simply passed it along to the logistics team and the "customer assembly line" continued from there.

The reason this disassociation needs to come to an immediate halt is because it lacks the continuity of a cohesive narrative. When you've purchased a product or service or even opted in for a free offer or lead magnet, the same messaging you've been exposed to throughout the buying process needs to be maintained through completion. This doesn't mean that your marketing team needs to head out to a customer's house and install their new HVAC unit but it does mean that your marketing team needs to help drive the fulfillment process in a way that maintains continuity with the global narrative of the sales funnel.

Anytime you connect content, you want to maintain continuity regardless of how small or large that connection is. The anchor text you use in a hyperlink should be a clear representation of what type of content the user should expect when they click on it. The title of your blog should clearly illustrate and help establish expectations as to what the user can expect if they read the blog. That's not to say you can't have fun, be creative and even be a little cryptic; you just have to do so within the confines of acceptable narrative practice.

This is especially true with social media marketing. You can maintain continuity and narrative while still being fun, playful and (in some cases) a little vague. "Do you know the top 7 fashion tips from the world's leading designers? #3 will blow you away!"—this is a great example of a clear call to action that isn't overly academic and still leaves room for (and even catalyzes) user curiosity.

INTUITIVE DECISIONS, DATA DRIVEN ADJUSTMENTS...

If I had asked people what they wanted, they would have said faster horses.

- Henry Ford

ONE OF THE MISTAKES WE MAKE AS DIGITAL MARKETERS IS PUTTING DATA before people. We become so obsessed with making data driven decisions that we forget that the data are driven by people. People are the catalysts and the data reflect the actions they have taken. As we work to empathize with our prospects, it's important that we trust our empathic reasoning. This is true even when (and sometimes especially when) our empathic reasoning doesn't necessarily coincide with the data.

The data can only measure that which is or has been—data can't be applied to anything other than what has already been tried. This means that anyone who makes 100% data driven decisions is limited to doing only what has already been done. There's an inability to innovate when you tie yourself too closely to data as a decision-making tool.

Please understand that I'm not saying you should ignore data. That is an equally catastrophic mistake. Data are an important indicator and worthy of ongoing reference and respect. I am saying however, that empathy trumps data in the creation process of digital marketing. Take what you know about your product or service, industry, Avatar, and value proposition and then make your decisions from a vantage point of empathy first.

The empathy first paradigm is meant to protect you from applying the sweeping rules and generalizations that accompany data driven decision making. Intuitive decisions will allow you to assume a "human first" paradigm that enables your campaigns to be successful much earlier and without the headache and heartache that accompanies the tedious task of taking templated marketing campaigns and attempting to test them into submission.

If a data driven decision paradigm were truly the best approach, there would be no need for digital marketers. Once a single product, service or industry has been successfully marketed, the only thing left to do would be to clone the campaigns and then sell them off to everyone in that industry. Intuitive decisions, while still informed by data and past experiences, force you to acknowledge the unknown and account for it using our single greatest marketing tool: empathy.

With all of that said, once the intuitive decisions have been made, it's very important to monitor their successes and failures and then make data driven adjustments. Starting with empathy ensures you'll position yourself for the greatest potential degree of acceptance by your Avatar. But once empathy has been thoroughly and effectively deployed, it's time to test your assumptions and determine what changes are necessary. This can only help to serve you not only with the campaign at hand but in all future campaigns as well.

Testing your assumptions in reference to intuitive decisions is a dangerous prospect for a lot of us because we tend to get romantic about them. When we empathize, we are utilizing an emotional utility to make a logical decision. It is easy for us to get emotional about that decision and then work to protect it. Intuitive decision making followed by data driven adjustments will help protect your campaigns from becoming templated and routine, and will also ensure any incorrect assumptions are identified and rectified.

As you make data driven adjustments, make sure you start paying attention to the "why." This is difficult to do because it requires you to make assumptions as to why the data is yielding the results you're seeing. Oftentimes this feels like chasing your tail. However, if you don't pay attention to the "why" and you simply follow the direction the data is pointing you in, you might not be making the right changes for the right reasons.

If you notice that your social media users are engaging with images far more than video, it's very easy to immediately assume that image based media appeals to your Avatar more and simply modify all your campaigns to reflect that new information. However, a smart marketer is going to look at the difference between the images and the videos and find out why one is performing better than the other prior to just trusting the data.

Do the images present more value up front than the videos do? If you're using an infographic, chart or graph in your imagery, you are immediately presenting data and value to your user without any precursor. If your video has the same information but a logo sting (introduction) on the front end you might be wasting the valuable few seconds a user takes to determine whether or not the video is going to be of any interest. What happens when you take the images that are performing well and make them the thumbnail for the video?

One of our Clients purchases homes from private sellers who want to skip the hassle of listing the home on the retail market. When reviewing the conversion metrics for his campaign, we noticed a very distinct difference between the phrases "sell my home" and "sell my house." Both phrases resulted in roughly the same number of leads and had almost the exact same cost per lead. However, the key phrase "sell my house" resulted in far more closed deals than the key phrase "sell my home" did.

Anecdotally, we believe this is because people who refer to their property as a "home" have a stronger psychological attachment to the property than people who use the word "house". Because of this attachment they are far less likely to sell. This type of data driven result is something we ultimately took and utilized across the rest of the campaign. It informed the entire content creation process site-wide. However, it required us to dig into the result and determine "why" instead of simply changing our bid structure to the higher value key phrase and moving on. It was an intuitive decision made from a data catalyst.

This is what separates bad from good and good from great digital marketers. Following data without understanding the human element associated with it will result in your backing yourself into corners and not understanding how you got there. If you know any statisticians you've heard the phrase "correlation isn't causation" probably more times than you would care to. That's fine and dandy for a math jockey but the job of the digital marketer is to find out what is causation and make educated assumptions based on the available data.

The decisions you make are going to impact the health and well-being of your marketing campaign. The worst decision you can ever make is no decision. Abdicating your decision making to the data driven model makes you no more valuable than a computer. In fact, you become less valuable than a computer because a computer at least has no proclivity for human error.

UNDERSTANDING A NETWORK

OFTEN, THE NEED TO EMPATHIZE CAN SURPASS THE TARGETING OF AN individual and can pertain to an entire group or demographic. This is especially true when we begin discussing social and other media networks that we use to advertise. It is extremely important that you spend time learning and understanding the culture and personality of a network. Not doing so will potentially put you at odds with the entire user base.

For example, Facebook as a tool is meant for staying up to date on relevant topics, connecting with people, relating on areas of common interest, discussing issues, voicing opinions and seeing other people's reactions. Instagram on the other hand is for dreaming, being inspired, goal setting and escaping. While the two networks are owned by the same company and often viewed as two arms to the same machine, their cultural outlay couldn't be more different.

I use this example specifically because the Facebook ad manager bundles Facebook and Instagram in a way that simply allows you to push your Facebook ads into Instagram. The inclusion is treated almost as an afterthought and, in my opinion, is a massive mistake. If you're creating ads that are well suited for Facebook users, then they aren't going to work on Instagram and vice versa.

This is equally true for organic social media posting. Often I see brands taking the exact same daily posts and simply cascading them across all social networks. They use a tool like Hootsuite and schedule the same post to each of their social profiles. Keep in mind, there's absolutely nothing wrong with this if your sole goal is to simply maintain a presence. However, if you are seeking to engage a user base, you need to do so on their terms.

If you've spent any time on Reddit, you should be more than aware that the network has an extremely distinct personality. Reddit has created an internet subculture all its own and making any attempts to artificially infringe upon that subculture is a recipe for almost guaranteed incessant and ongoing trolling from Redditors. Few people can survive the fury of an enraged Reddit audience and nothing stokes that fury more than people or companies attempting to use Reddit for anything other than what the user base feels it was created for.

LinkedIn is another network that has started to develop a very distinct personality. There are acceptable and expected manners of approaching a person or prospect that LinkedIn not only allows but actually monetizes. It can be an amazing tool for prospecting and reaching out directly to decision makers. At the same time, there are several LinkedIn marketing models that are reminiscent of batch and blast spam tactics that will quickly get you shunned by all but the most oblivious LinkedIn users.

Google Plus is a unique network with a very interesting personality in that it has none. Because how can you have a personality without people? [Sorry...I had to :-)] Jokes aside however, Google Plus did something that was revolutionary in some ways but actually might have been the cause of its poor adoption. Plus attempted to compartmentalize people's social circles in a way that would allow them to engage with various groups differently, as defined by the user.

I think the idea here is of immense value. Most of us have experienced the inner torment that comes with the Facebook friend request from your new Client. We tend to engage with each of our various circles differently which is why Google built the concept of these "circles" into Google Plus. The concept was sound but the compartmentalization also kept Google Plus from being able to develop its own culture or distinct personality.

Google essentially built a social networking tool that allowed other people to define their own communities. In this way Google might have simply put too much faith in its user base as it would appear people prefer to be given the opportunity to join a predefined community rather than attempt to define their own micro-communities. This sterilization of the network made for low engagement and, ultimately, low adoption.

Think about all the social tools you intend to use for marketing purposes and make sure you're approaching your initiatives from an empathic vantage point. Twitter, SnapChat and YouTube are distinct communities with distinct voices and personalities that need to be respected. Making an attempt at engaging with a community before learning their language is a recipe for disaster.

Cultural specification isn't limited to social media networks either. I've spent some time writing guest blogs for various publications and it has always served me well to spend some time looking at the publication in question and learning about the culture that has been built around it. There is a striking difference between the community at Search Engine Journal and the community at Moz.

That isn't to say that one is better than the other, simply that an intelligent marketer will take the time to acquaint him or herself with the network in question prior to attempting to insert themselves into the collective conversation. Once again, this is where empathy carries so much power. When you make an attempt at understanding what people have been acclimated to and what they expect, you position yourself for success when you begin your dialog.

Empathy should be a cornerstone approach for every new network with which you engage. If you ever find yourself sending an email to a new list, make sure you've spent some time learning who these new people are, what they're interested in, why they subscribed and what expectations they may have. One of our core strategies for new Clients is seeking out online networks with robust subscriber bases and paying for inclusion in their email blasts, typically with high value content.

This approach helps us to immediately connect with a very targeted Avatar through a trusted conduit in a way that brings value first. However, when we do this we make sure to learn as much as we can about the network we choose as well as their readers. We ask for historic emails to see what they have already been sent and also request usage data to try and get a sense as to what they might be interested in for the future.

When engaging with any online group or network, an empathic approach is vital to ensuring your acceptance. People tend to take ownership over these spaces and it's important that we learn to respect that. The same way you would try and honor any reasonable cultural expectations when you visit someone's home, you should spend the time and energy required to learn those same expectations for the online networks with which you engage.

APPLICATION SUGGESTIONS

EMPATHY NEEDS TO BE A FOUNDATIONAL PRINCIPLE OF HOW YOUR ORganization functions. In order for that to be true you'll need to build empathy into your day to day operations. It needs to be integrated into every process that is feasibly possible. Here are a few suggestions for making sure empathy gets the credit it deserves.

1. Go Method! Keep a Journal as Your Avatar

Start keeping a journal as though you are your own Avatar. Writing the journal in the first person will help you start to think like your Avatar. You should also try to write about situations, circumstances and topics that may not be directly related to your Avatar's business or buying experience. What's their home life like? What do they do for fun? What current news events might be affecting them?

Beginning to understand who your Avatar is as a person (instead of just a potential prospect) will yield invaluable results in terms of how best to approach them, what to say and how to say it. Empathy starts with the earnest need to understand another person. Journaling is a safe place to experiment with thoughts and ideas as to who they may be, what challenges they might be facing, what their value system is and ultimately who they are as a person.

This is going to get really touchy-feely for a moment but I truly believe what I'm about to say from the bottom of my heart: The natural result of empathy is love. If you are truly working to empathize with the people you are marketing to, you should find yourself loving them. When you really get to know someone, know their struggles, their hopes, their dreams, their values and what makes them tick, I contend that it's impossible not to feel something akin to love for them.

When you love someone, you want the best for them. If you truly feel that what you're offering is of value, it'll become easy for you to make that case. If you approach your prospects from a place of love, you'll be better equipped to serve them. You will have their best interests at heart and will ultimately earn their business because that level of connection and commitment truly cannot be faked.

Okay, hippie time is over weirdos. Let's move on...

2. Have an Avatar Advocate

Assign someone in your organization the task of being an advocate for your Avatar. This is especially helpful if you're serving multiple Clients and, by proxy, multiple Avatars. Spread the advocacy around and assign different people various Avatars to advocate for.

Try to assign them according to who might fit the best based on temperament, disposition, etc.

This person will assume the position of protecting the Avatar, especially when you're creating new material or building a campaign. They'll challenge every assumption and make sure that nothing is being done that isn't in the Avatar's best interest. If you're a fun crowd (and as digital marketers it should be safe to assume that you are) you could even do some improvised role play.

3. Be Your Avatar's Best friend

Okay, so this one isn't always feasible but if you can pull it off then there's just nothing better. Go make friends! Track down a handful of folks that are solid representations of your Avatar and do whatever you can to earn some of their time. Offer up a free meal or fun outing and get to know who they are as people. Make sure you're up front about what you're doing but don't let that be the purpose of the relationship. You aren't there to learn about what they do or even how they buy, you're there to learn about *who they are*.

4. Be Your Avatar

The only thing better than being your Avatar's best friend is being your Avatar. Again, this isn't always possible. If your Avatar is a Physician, then it's probably not feasible to attend a decade of medical school. However, if you're marketing a line of skin care products it might be an easy step for you to try and become a skin care product enthusiast.

Expand your horizons and stretch your comfort zone! Learn to play golf, travel, try new products, shop for a service, put yourself in the positions that your Avatar will ultimately be in and you will come back with experiences and information that you would never have had otherwise.

PRINCIPLE 2
BE THE FIRST (AND LAST) TO GIVE VALUE

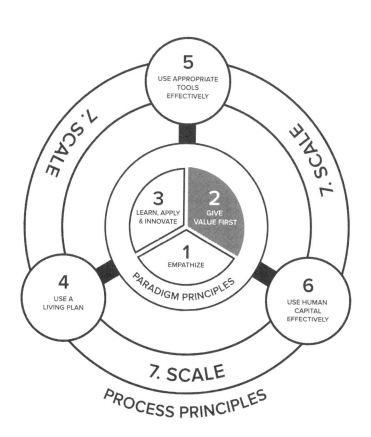

THERE'S NO QUANTIFIABLE FUTURE IN A TRANSACTIONAL RELATIONSHIP. I'M not saying that there's anything wrong with them. They work perfectly fine and, for the most part, are the established status quo of the economic world. But, for all intents and purposes, a transactional relationship has none of the qualities that we would hope to find in our long-term relationships.

You have a transactional relationship with a vending machine. You put money in and candy comes out. The exchange of value is 1 to 1. You have no loyalty to the vending machine and the vending machine has no further obligation to you. However, if the vending machine steals your money, it is a universally accepted rule that you be allowed to utilize every form of violence in existence until it yields what you are owed.

In many cases, this is how we conduct our business. If you pay me money I will clean your carpets (or print your business cards or build your website or watch your children). If you give me your time, I will give you a proposal. If you sign this contract bequeathing me your soul and first two children, I will be your attorney.

Don't be mistaken, transactional relationships aren't just limited to the analog world. If you give me your email address, I will give you my lead magnet. If you subscribe, I will send you updates. If you share, if you like, if you post, if you comment, etc. etc. etc.

With most transactional relationships, the contingency always rests with the prospect. They are responsible for catalyzing the relationship. What if you could change that sequence? What if you could catalyze a relationship with more prospects than you could ever possibly serve? What if I stopped asking annoying rhetorical questions and just got to the point?

The value first principle is built on the foundation that you are always going to be the first to provide value and that the value is provided without contingency. The second half of that sentence is equally as important as the first. You can't approach a value first paradigm with any level of expectation. There's no greater turn off than the "now you owe me" approach some marketers take. You need to want to provide value first because you want to help people, helping for helping's sake.

Something magical happens when you give value to people without any expectation of return— they start to trust you! Remember, digital marketing is relationship building. The value first principle is what starts your relationship off on the single most important principle of successful relationships: trust.

That's not to say that they'll trust you forever. You'll need to continue to prove yourself and earn greater degrees of trust as the relationship progresses (just like any relationship). However, the foundation of the relationship is no longer transactional. You have elevated the nature of the relationship to a higher purpose. What that purpose is will be defined by what you're offering.

Further, when you have earned the trust of your prospect, it places you in a position to be able to ask for things. That's not to say they're obligated to comply, just that, from a social etiquette perspective, you're better positioned to submit an "ask" and be met with a positive response.

I have heard Ryan Deiss of DigitalMarketer.com draw an analogy of this give/ask system to deposits and withdrawals in a bank account. You are allowed to make withdrawals against the relationship account that you keep with your prospects but never in excess of the amount of deposits that you have made. If you ever overdraw your account, you hurt and even potentially destroy, your relationship. And, it stands to reason that you need to make deposits first before you can ever make a withdrawal.

This is where the "value first" paradigm gets really, really interesting. What happens when your "ask" (your withdrawal) leads to even more value (more deposits) for your user? I call this approach "lock stepping your value" and it's an absolutely ninja way of earning new prospects, customers and advocates and keeping them for life.

LOCKSTEP VALUE

THE LOCKSTEP VALUE APPROACH IS THE MOST EFFECTIVE ASCENSION MODEL available to digital marketers. Essentially, you're using value to prove concept and then calling upon the trust earned from that transaction to prove further value. Here's an example of a lockstep value process:

[queue sitcom flashback sequence]

Spartacus is a CPA. His Avatar is the owner or manager of small to medium sized manufacturing companies in the Southwestern United States.

Spartacus writes an amazing blog on how manufacturing companies should structure their income accounts. He explains how certain types of costing can drastically impact the company's long-term balance sheet and help mitigate short term tax liability. The blog includes a very easy to follow, step-by-step process for setting up this account structure. As you have probably already guessed, Spartacus has given value first here without any expectation of return.

In my experience, most digital marketers would have preferred to present a synopsis of this altered practice, a simple breakdown of the value proposition, and then turned the actual "how to" into a lead magnet that the user would trade for their email. There's nothing technically wrong with this approach but this is transactional. There's a value for value exchange (the email for the content) and it results in no real trust or relationship building.

Instead Spartacus chose to divulge everything up front and utilize this "give" as a "deposit" into the relationship account with his potential prospects. There's no expectation of further action or reciprocity which places Spartacus in a position of trust with his prospects. He's not only a thought leader, he's also someone who has provided measurable and tangible value.

Now that the user has engaged with Spartacus's online property, there are quite a few options available to us. First, we can offer a very soft but clear call to action within the provided content. This doesn't compromise our "give" (the content) as long as the content is complete and actionable, and the subsequent call to action isn't required in order to experience the value. For instance, as the prospect is reading the article, we can offer them an excel worksheet that they can use to put the practices detailed in the article to work. It's a supplement to the content (which helps maintain the continuity of the funnel) but not a requirement for value.

Further, this offering is far more valuable than what we're asking in return for it. The worksheet is a functional utility that Spartacus could very easily expect to charge for. In fact, a cursory search of his competitive market yields results that speak to that fact: the vast majority of his competitors who have similar products are billing for them. This is where we begin to practice the second half of the principle, to also be the last to provide value.

Spartacus was the first to provide value (the article), put forth his "ask" which was the prospects email and then followed up with even more value which is the excel worksheet. He has effectively book-ended his value by being the first and the last to provide value which means his deposits will always exceed his withdrawals. He'll continue this paradigm throughout the entire relationship.

Pro Tip: *The CTA doesn't need to reside on the page alone. Now that the user has engaged with his digital property, Spartacus pixels them through various networks (Google, YouTube, Facebook, etc.) and can now remarket his subsequent offer, the worksheet, to the user throughout their future web browsing experience. Typically, a very small percentage of users are going to convert on the first ask. However, a subtle remarketing campaign can quantify these numbers on an exponential scale if the value you're offering is truly relevant.*

Now that the user has provided his or her email address (the first "ask" Spartacus has made in the relationship) he'll send them the worksheet that he promised. Here's where I like to double down on the value first paradigm. Instead of just sending them the worksheet, Spartacus sends them the worksheet and a completely free video training course on how to utilize the worksheet. He never made mention of this training course in his initial "ask" and is giving it to the user without any additional cost or expectation.

A few things happen here, not only is Spartacus amplifying the amount of trust he's earning in the eyes of his prospect, he's also teaching his prospect that Spartacus is the type of person that will always over-deliver. This neuro-association, when built properly, is going to make every subsequent "ask" that Spartacus makes more effective. His prospects are going to be all too eager to give Spartacus whatever it is he's asking for because they know they're going to get even more value than he's promising in return.

Now the prospect has benefited from the original article, they have the worksheet and they have the training videos. For all this value Spartacus has asked only for the prospect's first name and email address. As it stands, he was the first to give value, the last to give value **and** the value he gave was many multiples more than the prospect was expecting. Spartacus is in a great position to submit his next ask.

[Note to my DM purists: I'm skipping some best practices here, specifically the indoctrination campaign and possible value optimizations/ascension models, not because they're not awesome but because they're not necessary to explaining the value first concept. Forgive me... or don't. Just know that I know what you were thinking.]

Spartacus sends a soft engagement email campaign. The first email starts off by asking the prospect what they think of the worksheet and training videos. He might include a few pro tips he has collected from working with other companies, nothing immense or earth shattering. Just a few "one liner" data points that might amplify the value of his tool ever further. He can also follow up with additional value by asking questions about their experience. Are they having any issues? Do they have any questions he can answer? Etc.

Within the engagement sequence, even at the end of the first email, Spartacus can now submit his next "ask." If the prospect has found value in the approach that Spartacus offers, the worksheet he created and the video series he gave, they might also find an immense amount of value in a complete evaluation of their books by one of Spartacus's expert staff members.

He goes on to explain that he and his staff have over 10 years in the business of helping manufacturing companies with their bookkeeping, accounting and taxes. They have a proprietary 25-point audit that has saved some of the companies he has worked with millions of dollars. A few examples of this social proof are very impactful at this point. There's no work required on the prospect's side whatsoever. The prospect only needs to provide Spartacus's team with access to the previous year's tax return and his or her current bookkeeping system.

An audit like this from competing firms could easily cost four and sometimes even five figure sums. Spartacus is willing to provide this audit for the flat fee of $497. There's absolutely zero obligation once the audit is complete. The prospect will receive the complete audit with nothing held back and is free to use it however they see fit. Further, Spartacus offers a 100% money back guarantee. If the prospect doesn't feel that the audit provided the value they were expecting, Spartacus will refund 100% of the purchase price, no questions asked.

Once again, the value associated with this "ask" is so staggeringly weighted in the prospect's favor that it is an absolute no brainer. Keep in mind, these approaches may not all be right for your business. For example, you might not be equipped to offer a 100% money back guarantee. That's perfectly fine. But remember that you aren't trying to make money here. You are trying to offer as much value as possible in exchange for a sum that will ensure that you simply don't lose any money.

When someone buys something from you once, they become increasingly more likely to purchase from you a second time; and every purchase they make increases the likelihood of a subsequent purchase. (success.adobe.com 2015) The point in this very first transaction isn't to make tons of money, but instead is to acclimate your prospect to spending money with you. You're working yourself into their mental positioning as an "approved vendor."

You'll also notice something very important about this "ask" — it's going to set Spartacus up to provide immense amounts of future value. The audit is an amazing launch pad for recommending future services and engagement points and doing so with the historical substantiation of the prospect's own books. He's basically being paid to spend time determining where and how he might best be equipped to serve this prospect.

Now the delivery of the audit puts Spartacus in an excellent position to provide additional value at virtually no expense. He can provide the Client with the promised audit as well as action items the Client can take away for a few quick wins. This is yet another example of how Spartacus continues to provide more value than promised.

From this point, the process will continue on a custom basis based upon the needs of the Client. However, the paradigm never changes. Spartacus will always provide value first, provide more value than expected when possible, never withdraw more than he has deposited, and ensure he's always the last to have provided value.

Using this process Spartacus has worked himself into a position of being a valued and trusted source of information. Further, he has done so before he has engaged the prospect with a core offer. This makes a substantial difference in the sales process because it equips him to approach the larger ticket items he may want to offer the Client from a position of strength. From this point I hope you'll agree that he is positioned to be wildly successful with this new Client.

When approaching your relationship building with a deposit/withdrawal paradigm, it's important to remember what constitutes a withdrawal. Money isn't the only thing you can withdraw from a prospect or Client. Anytime you ask for a Client's time you are making a withdrawal. When you ask for information or feedback, you may be making a withdrawal. When you ask for a referral or testimonial you are making a withdrawal. All of these are perfectly acceptable practices and nothing you need to avoid. Simply make it a habit to ensure that your deposits always exceed your withdrawals and that you are the first and last to make a deposit at any given point.

MARKETING IN A SILO

ONE OF THE MOST EXCITING BENEFITS OF THE VALUE FIRST PARADIGM IS THE fact that it takes the users out of a buying cycle and puts them into your own personal marketing silo. Using the example of Spartacus again, do you think his prospects are ever going to be hitting the Google machine and looking for "best CPAs for manufacturing companies?" No! They're heavily engaged with his content and specific offerings in a way that negates the need for them to conduct a search. Using this approach you are able to preempt the need for a provider search by using value based ascension.

You're no longer competing against other potential providers. Now, instead of value propositions being written in a way that are meant to differentiate you from other providers, your value propositions can be written in a way that properly qualifies your prospect against the service. This helps your prospects appropriately funnel themselves against your available services without you having to risk losing them to a competitor simply because the competitors are vaguer in their messaging.

Obviously, this isn't always the case. But even in the circumstances where you are competing against other providers, the value-added approach puts you in a far more likely position to catalyze engagement than a provider who is attempting a more transactional approach or arrangement.

Here's a real-life example of how the lockstep value approach and marketing in a silo helped a longtime Client completely side-step the commoditization of his industry:

When we started working with this Client, a very well respected nutritionist, he was already running moderately successful pay-per-click campaigns that were generating a fair amount of relatively well qualified leads. The issue he was facing was that his primary call to action, a free consultation, was extremely cost and time prohibitive for him and inhibited his ability to scale his business.

In the world of high end nutrition consulting, this free consult was the industry standard and something that virtually every one of his competitors was offering. He had toyed with scaling it back or utilizing different offers but nothing was working and his experiments simply hurt his lead flow.

An interesting aside to the value first paradigm is an industry's ability to commoditize something past the point of being valuable and to the point of being a reasonable expectation. Once this level of commoditization has taken place, you can't include whatever it is that has been commoditized as the same level of deposit in your value first approach. This is no longer a "give" as much as it is a standard step in the established sales process.

I imagine in its infancy the automobile sales industry probably didn't offer test drives as a standard step in the process of buying a car. The vast majority of people couldn't drive and even among those that were buying automobiles drivers were typically employed to operate them. A test drive wasn't necessary. However, as the industry became more competitive and sales people looked for opportunities to provide differentiation, I can see how test drives became inexpensive ways of driving a user further down the sales funnel.

Can you imagine buying a car today without a test drive? (Incidentally, I plan on eating these words. There are some exciting things happening in the realm of online car buying.) Or buying something from a department store without knowing you could return it? Or ordering a pizza without the ability to have it delivered? Each of these was a value add that eventually turned into a standard piece of the core product purchase. This is part of the natural evolution of any industry, and in many cases something we all need to match some level of compliance against.

However, in quite a few cases these "understood" steps in your sales cycle could be drastically inhibiting your ability to scale, or could be simply hurting your profit margins. While there isn't always a "fix" to this problem, you can very often use the lockstep value approach to completely sidestep it! That's exactly what we did for our nutritionist.

We started with using high value content offerings to: a) elevate the conversation he was having with his prospects higher in the sales funnel and b) catalyze a value first approach that would enable him to earn the trust of his prospects and start providing immense amounts of value very early on. Keep in mind that this only works when you increase the amount of value that you're providing a prospect earlier in the purchasing lifecycle.

To empathize with a potential prospect's position, why would I even consider a nutritionist who didn't offer the same value added service that every single other equally qualified nutritionist was willing to offer completely free of cost? The answer is that the first nutritionist had already provided me with so much value that I was either stalled or completely stopped from searching for other nutritionists.

Using the same approach that I outlined above with our CPA Spartacus, we built funnels that utilized the value first paradigm through extremely high value content and media offerings to continue to convert our prospects further down the sales funnel. Prospects were engaged with very thorough "how to" content that spoke to specific needs and lifestyles. We were able to segment prospects as they engaged with our content in order to speak to them with greater degrees of specificity. And, above all, we were able to provide greater amounts of value up front when compared to his competitors.

By the time prospects reached the consultative conversion phase, the deposits we had made far outweighed the "ask" of a small fee for the initial consult. Before, our nutritionist was dealing with cold prospects who went searching for his service and had absolutely no information with which to make a decision—the industry standard free consult was an absolute necessity for their decision making process. However, when we were able to engage them earlier in the sales cycle and then provide extremely valuable and actionable content to drive them down the funnel, we positioned our Client to charge a fair and reasonable fee for the consult based off the amount of value he had already shown.

This fee not only helped our nutritionist justify his time, it also helped us to qualify prospects and ensure the leads we were driving were of an adequate value in terms of their willingness to spend. In addition, the initial consult was exponentially more valuable than it used to be because our nutritionist knew so much more about his new Patients than he had before. This was based solely on the content journey we had been tracking them through as they traveled down the funnel.

The full disclosure I'll make is that we still offered our recommended three tier guarantee:

1. Nothing was held back from the initial consult, nor was there any further obligation for additional services.
2. If they chose to engage our Nutritionist for further services, the cost of the initial consult could be used as a credit.
3. After the consult was complete, if they felt that the value didn't meet and exceed the amount they paid, our nutritionist would refund 100% of their purchase price, no questions asked.

As I said earlier, some or all the above may not always be feasible. However, I'm sure you can see that it completely destroys any potential objections a prospect may have about signing on for the initial engagement. If you truly believe in your product/service, then you shouldn't have any issue crafting your own high level satisfaction guarantee.

This approach worked phenomenally well for our Nutritionist. The amount of leads he had to service decreased (which was a good thing in this instance) and the number of qualified leads more than doubled. Because he was being compensated for the time he needed to spend with these new patients, he was able to scale his business.

He began bringing on junior associates to help him handle new patient intake, something he could have never afforded to do when the multitude of consults he was providing were all being done for free. Further, the value of the free consults was amplified drastically. Now he could afford to spend real quality time with his new patients and do so with far more context since they had previously been engaging with his funnel.

Keep in mind that this isn't something he ever could have done if he didn't begin providing value first and earlier in the sales cycle. Imagine if he attempted to bill for the same initial consult that every other nutritionist was offering for free. He would have died on the vine or been forced back into the free consult model.

Now that I've beaten that drum as hard as I can, allow me to be the hypocrite that I am and offer a note of caution for a moment: be very careful when you're marketing in a silo to ensure that you don't do anything that will be perceived as unfair or dishonest if your prospect ever happens to peek outside of said silo. Yes, our nutritionist was absolutely able to bill for a consult that his competitors were giving away for free. However, we were also able to effectively provide far more value up front than the competition and we worked very hard to illustrate how the consult's value was greatly amplified by how much we already knew about the prospect's specific needs.

The point I'm making is that our prospects would (hopefully) not feel cheated if they found out that there are nutritionists who offer a free consult when they had paid for ours. We had worked extremely hard to provide immense amounts of value up front, build trust, prove thought leadership and, ultimately, earn the ability to ask for reasonable compensation for a service that was obviously worth more than they were going to pay. All of that coupled with an out of this world satisfaction guarantee and we were well positioned to defend our decision.

However, had we simply used our marketing silo to enable us to bill for something that was very obviously the same type of product or service as was available elsewhere for free (or for less money), we would have found ourselves in an indefensible position. If you have ever paid for something that you later saw elsewhere for substantially less, you know the feeling of betrayal that is accompanied with that realization. All trust is lost in an instant and the relationship is shattered.

With that said, the silo should be used to amplify value up to a point that justifies potential higher prices or additional "asks." It is never meant to mask the lack of value of a product or service or hide the commoditization of a product/service in the marketplace. Sadly, this isn't always the case, but in the value first paradigm it should be.

IF YOU CAN'T START WITH MORE VALUE...

SOMETIMES THE ABILITY TO PROVIDE MORE VALUE EARLIER JUST DOESN'T exist. I've seen this problem in the general dental industry. We have quite a few Clients that provide specialty dental services (all-on-four, veneers, sedation dentistry, etc.) with which we have been extremely successful. These industries are great examples of thought leadership being established and capitalized upon to provide value and earn trust. However, in the realm of general dentistry that's not always the case.

If you live in a major metro, you have probably seen a million or so dentists and dental groups offering extremely aggressive promotions for new and first time patients. I have seen dentists offering a free initial consult, full cleaning & dental exam, x-rays and teeth whitening for $39. It should be obvious that the dentist is losing his shirt and his lab coat on the deal.

This deal would make sense if the dentists could count on a solid retention rate from their new patients. The initial visit would be considered a loss leader that could be justified by the intake of a new, long-term patient. Nothing could be further from the truth. Not only are these patients hard to retain, it's difficult to even get them to show up! Even after they've paid, a lot of these initial consults end up being no-shows. That's how negligible the up-front costs are, in that they are merely impulse buys that people later forget about.

Now, I'm not saying I have the end all solution for this problem. I honestly believe that the dental industry is just too saturated in some areas and that this is a byproduct of market saturation. However, I do believe there are things that can be done to help mitigate these factors and continue the relationship with a lockstep value approach.

Returning to our first principle of empathy for just a moment, remember the importance and impact that narrative as a concept has on people. I think one of the most impactful things a dentist can do in this instance is to begin a narrative with these new patients. Starting the narrative provides even more value and requires the patient to commit to the process.

I have outlined my advice for digital marketers who are working for or with dentists that are in this position. If you don't mind my saying, it's ninja.

When your new discount patient comes in, start a timeline for them and let them know about it. If you're doing periodontal charting, you're already doing this. Now you're just going to make your patient aware of it and start to set goals for subsequent visits. Show the patient their problem areas (their 3, 4 and 5 scores) and explain to them what they mean. Then give them very clear instructions on what they need to do to improve these scores. This means sending them home with a tip sheet or checklist, something they can tape to their bathroom mirror.

Before they leave, make sure to set some reasonable goals for improvement. Let them know that you'd like the 5s to be 4s, the 4s to be 3s, etc., in the next six months. Obviously, the goal needs to be adjusted so it's reasonable for each specific patient. Write these goals down on the checklist that you're sending home with them.

If you want to get super ninja with it, you'll have multiple checklists for the three or five (or fifty) most common cases and you'll create an automated email nurture for each one of these segments as well. You'll drop these new patients into the nurture segment that you built to speak to their situation and they'll begin receiving updates, reminders and tips on making sure they accomplish their goals.

Pro Tip: *if you're using a tool like Infusionsoft (yes, I'm an Infusionsoft junkie and Certified Partner) you can actually insert custom data like the goals you discussed with the patient that then use snippets to include that data into the emails!*

Okay—here's where we get super-duper ninja in lock-stepping our value—most people are acclimated to seeing the dentist once every six months. Even if they don't do it, they're probably familiar with that timeline. At the end of the evaluation, your dentist is going to tell them that making sure they reach their goals is extremely important to him/her, so much so that they'd like to see the patient back in three months instead of six to make sure they're on track. And because this is an accelerated timeline, we're not going to charge them for this additional check-up.

How's that for additional value? The patient came in expecting a cleaning and instead got a comprehensive plan for oral health that included a personalized goal setting session and a free follow up appointment! Just wait until the patient starts getting the email nurture sequence that speaks to specific needs and goals. And, when the patient comes in for a second appointment, the dentist is going to put the second piece of the narrative into the periodontal chart. Make absolutely sure that the patient is privy to the connection in the phases and, once again, set some goals for the next appointment.

Guess who is never going to a different dentist ever again?

Here's the point of this little story, if you can't *start* with a silo, end with one. If you're in an industry or a position where there's no way to differentiate yourself up front, then differentiate yourself after the fact. It's harder, there's no denying that. In fact, it's so much harder that as a service provider I sometimes avoid industries where we're not able to make front-end impacts to the funnel. Not that there's anything wrong with these businesses, there's just so much more low hanging fruit when you happen to be the greatest digital marketer on the planet :-P

Another important note I'd like to offer up about the example I just provided: Very little of what we discussed was actually "digital" marketing. While we did supplement with an automated email nurture, the entire conversation centered on patients' experiences after they had already come into the office. This speaks to what I wrote about earlier in terms of the expansion of the sales funnel.

The necessity for continuity and a holistic user experience has expanded the digital marketer's reach well past the first few steps in the sales funnel. Because we're defining the narrative and driving global conversions, we've become responsible for the entire funnel. This is true even past the purchasing phase and into fulfillment and long-term nurture. The customer's experience is our domain, regardless of where it happens.

You may have some Clients push back on this concept. They'll assert that your job is to drive the leads and they'll take it from there. They might even tell you that they can't afford to take this type of approach because of the additional time required with each patient. If they had an approach that was already working, their argument would stand. However, if they're burning through new patients and seeing a low retention, they can't afford **not** to take action. Regardless, you'll find that some Clients refuse to allow you to influence larger scale business decisions.

My honest opinion? Dump these Clients. They're not only going to limit what you're capable of doing for them from a performance perspective but they're also going to limit your ability to grow as a digital marketer through the services you provide. You'll spend so much time, effort and energy on campaigns that you'll ultimately have little control over the business.

Set yourself up for success and work with people who understand that digital marketers are the quarterbacks of the customer experience team. I need to stop writing about this now because I just made a sports analogy. I'm a super nerd, not a football nerd—I have no idea where that came from.

SOCIAL PROOF IS THE NEW BRAND RECOGNITION

BRANDING USED TO BE THE END ALL BE ALL THE MARKETING WORLD. TO have a well-respected and recognizable brand was the epitome of marketing success. But now...

Social proof is more important than brand recognition.

I just pissed off a few people. I'm going to say it again: social proof is more important than brand recognition.

Incidentally, social proof is any type of public customer feedback you can use to help build your brand and validate purchase decisions. Testimonials, product reviews, case studies and video recommendations are all excellent examples of social proof. Social proof can also include less concrete messaging, such as comments on your blogs, thank you messages on your social media page and positive mentions on other people's online properties.

Now, keep in mind that I'm not saying that branding is no longer important. I didn't say that. What I am saying is that what people are saying about your brand is more important than whether or not people immediately recognize it. The entire Google algorithm is built on the concept of peer review. The internet is built around our relationship to and with other people. When other people are saying positive things about your company, brand, product, service, whatever, it makes a massive impact.

Think about your own buying experience. How often have you found a potential service provider that you subsequently Googled to see how well they're perceived in the market? Do the reviews you see on their company end up being one of the deciding factors in whether you use them? Of course!

By building social proof, you are building the equivalent of a national brand. When you can get people to speak positively and with passion about your company and the offering you provide, there's very little in the way of market positioning that can compete with that. We already know that, all other things being equal, the company with the most amount of visible social proof will win. What we need to wrap our heads around is that social proof will be the positive deciding factor even when all other things aren't equal.

Social proof will empower you to charge more, be selective about with whom you work and opt out of industry standards that other companies might be forced to hold to (like free consultations). It places you in the position of sought after instead of seeker. That's not to say you should charge more for the sake of it, but that you can justify charging more because the available public narrative helps to establish the increased value you provide.

WHY SOCIAL PROOF IS RELEVANT...

WHILE THE TOPIC IS OFF-TOPIC TO A DEGREE, THE VALUE FIRST PARADIGM is the absolute best catalyst to collecting positive social proof. When you are giving people immense amounts of value, and you are doing so without the implied expectation of reciprocity, you'll start to see the magic of social proof begin to materialize. People will do what people do when they're online: they'll talk!

You'll begin to see brand mentions, positive social media & blog comments, testimonials and sometimes even entire blogs written about the value you are providing. In some instances, you'll be well positioned to even ask for some of these. One of my favorite things to do when I provide a free video training series is, at the end of each video, just tell people that if they have received any value from the content I have produced to please make a video of their own telling people about it. You will be shocked at how many people do it!

What's really cool (and a total ninja move) is that in some instances you can request social proof and make it a give instead of an ask! If you already have a solid online following or really established list, here's a great offer you can push out that helps you build social proof and provides value to your prospect at the same time:

"Do you want to be featured [on our blog/in our next email blast/ on our page/etc.]? Send me a quick note or video telling me about how we've helped your business and we'll send it out in the next blast."

Once again, you'll be absolutely shocked at the responses you get. The more value you provide for people the more enthusiastic they'll be with their responses.

A few notes on maintaining an online reputation and building social proof:

Some of what is entailed in building social proof can be automated. Once you've put the mechanisms in play to request social proof they'll function in perpetuity and slowly help you aggregate a broad catalog of amazing reviews and testimonials you can use across all your digital properties. There are a myriad of tools available to assist in this endeavor: Google, Yelp, Shopper Approved, etc.

The interesting thing about online reputation management is that (as the title states) it needs to be managed. If you leave your reputation at the mercy of the "powers that be" there's a massive risk in not being able to control any negative feedback you may end up having. Sadly, positive experiences are not reported on quite as fervently as negative experiences. Having a large collection of organic and positive ratings will help ensure that any negative ratings you experience are seen against a far more forgiving backdrop.

Pro Tip: *I believe one of the best ways to manage negative reviews is to make sure you're always in front of them. We built an automated customer feedback tool for a home services Client of ours that we now use for ourselves and multiple other Clients. Whenever a service is complete, an email goes out to the Customer within a day or two. The email asks the customer whether or not they're happy with the service they received and offers them two links to choose from: "yes"/"no." You can even get playful and use a happy face/sad face.*

If they select "no" then they're immediately taken to a brief form that asks something to the effect of "How can we make this right?" That form is directed to the department manager for immediate action. The benefit to having this system in place is that you have taken an unhappy customer and given him/her a place to vent frustration. Instead of taking to the internet and pontificating negative opinions, the clients have relieved themselves (however slightly) of that pressure and given you or your Client the opportunity to fix the issue.

If they select "yes" they're taken to a landing page that thanks them for their feedback; oftentimes you can even include a coupon for future services. The next day the "yes" respondents receive a soft request for a testimonial with links to the various networks they can choose from. You'll find that some customers might have a preference in regards to where they write their reviews. Don't limit your ability to capture positive customer feedback by being stubborn about where you're collecting it!

THE VALUE OF VALUABLE CONTENT

ONE OF THE MAJOR PARADIGM SHIFTS WE NEED TO REPEATEDLY REINFORCE in ourselves as well as others, is the value in valuable content. There's a reason I'm being a little redundant here. Writing content because you think you need to is worthless. If you're producing content just to populate a blog or make sure you have fresh content available to be crawled, if the purpose of your content isn't to provide value through thought leadership, then you are wasting everyone's time.

Content for the sake of content is the scourge of the internet. There is truly no upside. It is rarely going to be seen since it's of very little value and, even when it is seen, it'll only show you in a poor light because it's of very little value. When you create content, you need to do so from the vantage point that this might be the very first and very last impression you will ever make on a prospect before they make a decision. It needs to be knock-their-socks-off good. I love what Rand Fishkin has to say about 10x content: Your content needs to be 10 times better than anything else out there.

The internet is nothing more than a conduit for content dissemination. Its very reason for existence is to house and transmit the content that you're building. Content is not only important, it is the single most important facet of your digital strategy. I am always completely blown away when I see how people treat the content creation process. I can't begin to count the number of Clients we have had over the years that had no problem paying high five and six figure sums for a website from some "creative agency" but would scoff at paying a fraction of that for content creation for a site, incidentally, that was being built for the sole purpose of housing the content!

So, valuable content is the only content you should be creating, capiche? That means that you need to start valuing your valuable content. Business owners tend to look at their blogs, white papers, eBooks and other forms of potentially free media as worthless. They're just the bait that is being used to attract eyes to our site. Once attracted, the real trade in value will start with stuff that's actually valuable. This is flawed thinking. Your content is of immense value. You are providing an amazing service by delivering your thought leadership to a group of people for which it is directly applicable.

The reason I'm working so hard to make this point is: if you're going to attempt to operate with a "give value first" paradigm, it is important that you value what you're giving. Otherwise you're going to kill yourself trying to front load your prospects with just way too much "stuff." The content you are creating has very real and intellectually tangible value. If you don't recognize that you'll have a difficult time convincing other people of it. Sometimes the most valuable thing we can provide someone who has a complex question is a simple answer.

Start thinking of the content you are creating as a paid subscription. Begin to see yourself as the editor of a respected and sought after publication that people pay monthly to receive. Truly try to imagine that you're going to be held to those standards of quality. This will do two things for you—the first is that it will ensure the content you allow to pass into publication is good enough to put in front of paid subscribers. The second is that it'll put you in the correct frame of mind, which is that the content you are producing is so good it's worth paying for.

And, by the way, you are being paid for your content. You're being paid in the attention of your target Avatars. If you don't think that's way more valuable than a monthly subscription fee, I would like to invite you to punch yourself in the face. I have heard Gary Vaynerchuk say on multiple occasions that, at the end of the day, the only thing he really *does* is day trade attention.

The attention of your Avatar is the absolute most valuable thing of which you could possibly be in possession. In fact, in terms of long-term returns, it is even more valuable than an engagement with that very same Avatar. Imagine two competing companies, Company A and Company B. Company A has an existing engagement with Aaron the Avatar, meaning he is currently their Client. But Company B has Aaron's focused attention. He's reading their blogs, subscribing to receive their emails and actively engaging with their content. Who do you think is ultimately going to be Aaron's long-term service provider?

Earning a prospect's business is obviously important. But to keep their business you need to keep their attention. This is done in many ways. The most effective and scalable is through high value content. Regardless of the type of business you are currently in, realize that you are now also in the content business. Whatever it is that you do, whatever service you provide, demographic you serve, industry you operate in, you need to become one of the most prolific content creators within your chosen vertical. And if you're performing digital marketing services on behalf of a larger Client base, you need to help your Clients get there too.

Value first does not necessarily have to mean content, but I challenge you to find something more scalable and ubiquitously valuable. In some way or another, content is the magic key to the hearts and minds of every single purchasing base a digital marketer has the ability to impact. It's at the epicenter of our industry and will dictate our ability to survive and thrive. Content, incidentally, doesn't have to be written content. Videos, infographics, swipe files, checklists, and excel calculators are all "content."

And if you aren't a content creator, find one! Hire one, align with one, partner with one, trade with one, outsource to one. Find a rock star content creator and never, ever take them for granted. But, if you take this route, remember that you can only outsource content creation, you can't outsource thought leadership. The better the content creator you're outsourcing to, the better your content will be (obviously) but no amount of research on a topic can replace a thought leader.

THOUGHT LEADERSHIP AND CONTENT REPURPOSING

This is one of the single biggest problems I have ever faced as a digital marketer, in terms of performing services on behalf of other people. When we're marketing for ourselves, thought leadership should come relatively naturally. If you're a competent practitioner, you already know your service, your space and your market. However, when you start to build digital marketing campaigns on behalf of someone else, the lines begin to blur. When asking Clients for content direction, I have heard more often than I care to remember, "That's what I hired you for!"

I have amazing content creators on staff and we have been able to pull off some truly astounding feats of content creation. We build content for engineers charged with large scale military manufacturing jobs, medical device industries, professional services and dog toys. There's not a topic I would be afraid to tackle given the extraordinary team we've been able to assemble. However, no matter how good your writers are you still need to find a way to get your Client to assume the role of thought leader.

No amount of research will ever replace the value that a thought leader can bring to the table. The benefit is that you don't need an exceptional amount of time or information in order to properly point your muzzle. While information can be researched, your Client's specific opinions, feelings, approach and experience is something you need to commit to getting from them if you're going to produce 10x content. Without the unique perspective of an expert, you are left simply repackaging what you can find through research which doesn't provide much, if any, unique value.

I realize that this isn't what we want to hear, precisely because it is so painfully hard to get our Clients to cooperate with these types of initiatives. I recommend a few approaches when you're working with delegated thought leadership:

Build an Information Pass Down Routine and Make It Easy!

We have several Clients that provide us with regular videos. A lot of them just record themselves talking on their morning commute. They'll record a video of themselves speaking to a topic, news event, product or service but they do so with a deep dive paradigm that gives our writers the context they need to provide immense amounts of value.

In many cases, the topic comes from a content schedule we built into their marketing plan or a specific need we have identified. In other instances, the Client decides they want to speak to something specific. Regardless of where the idea comes from, the thought leadership needs to come from the thought leader. What's great is that, once they've provided even just a few minutes of context, your writers are empowered to fill in the blanks through research and competitive analysis.

If you have Clients that aren't comfortable with videos, have them send in voice recordings. There are a ton of apps available that allow people to make and share extended voice notes. I have found that these aren't quite as effective as video. When people know they're being recorded they tend to be more animated and enthusiastic about the topic.

Provide a Lot of Options and Long-term Visibility

Regardless of whether or not you're doing this yourself or you're helping a Client build their own pass down process, you need to ensure that there are options available from a topical standpoint. It's easy to feel blocked or creatively stifled when we're forced to speak to one specific topic. It helps to have a small list of potential topics one can choose from. I like to keep a Google document for each of our Clients that has a running list of content needs and requests. Clients can access this and then pick from the prioritized list.

It is also important to make sure there is visibility in terms of the topics for which you are requesting thought leadership. Because you "don't know what you don't know," there may be redundancies, interdependencies, contradictions or unnecessary overlap that occurs between certain topics. A thought leader would be able to review a list of needs and help you to understand what is and is not necessary. The important part of enabling this ability is making sure that you do the work up front and have a comprehensive list of required content if and when possible.

Repurpose Your Content

Your thought leader is, by nature, a very busy person. In small companies, it is almost always one of the owners or managing directors and in medium sized companies it tends to be the more tenured technicians with the most amount of experience. Because of how valuable their time is, you need to work to amplify and quantify the information they are giving you.

The best way to do this is through content repurposing and amplification. Many articles can very easily be turned into an infographic. Infographics can typically be spliced up and turned into slide shows. Slide shows can easily be placed on a timeline with a voice over added to it and turned into a video. A collection of articles can be combined to create a white paper. Some email announcements can be repurposed into press releases and most press releases can be re-written to create great on-site content.

Regardless of how you choose to repurpose, if you're not getting a wealth of content from each interview or video your Client provides then you aren't making effective use of their time. Every medium of content provides the opportunity of communicating a thought in a different way. Take advantage of these opportunities and amplify the content you already have through every single available channel!

THE AFTER-VALUE VALUE

WE HAVE ALREADY DISCUSSED BEING THE FIRST AND LAST TO GIVE. THIS concept of "book-ending" your value will ensure that the ongoing deposits you are making into the relationship you're cultivating will continue to be viewed favorably and through a "value driven" lens.

The issue is that being the last to give is not always as simple as it may seem. In some instances, there aren't any additional steps in a process. The new Client has been value optimized and ascended as far and high as they're going to go. In these instances, it's important not to abandon them or go silent. They're used to a constant value stream and stopping this value stream once they've completed a purchasing cycle will do nothing but illustrate the fact that your intentions were only ever to get them to buy from you. If a Client of yours ever feels this way, the relationship you have built is next to worthless.

While there may not be much monetary value in continuing to nurture the relationship of a Client that has already purchased everything they're going to purchase from you, these can still rank among your most important Clients! Because they have completed your sales cycle from start to finish, it stands to reason that you have a stronger relationship with them than you do with other Clients. They know you and trust you and, if you allow them the opportunity, they will become your biggest advocates.

Is there a greater opportunity for a digital marketer than to be given the chance to serve someone who knows that we no longer stand to benefit from them? Not only does this allow you to earn an enormous amount of goodwill but it also changes the dynamic in terms of how you can communicate with this Client and what you're able to ask of them. When you continue to make deposits with Clients that have nowhere else to go in your sales cycle, it doesn't mean that you shouldn't make withdrawals against those deposits; it just means the nature of the withdrawals change.

Imagine having a focus group that knew you, trusted you and was your exact Avatar. That's exactly what you have created with these "end of the line" users. You can utilize your available "asks" for a myriad of strategic needs and you'll find that the value you receive is immense. One of my absolute favorite things to do with this type of user is single question surveys. I like to add these as a rider to value driven emails. I tend to ask questions about the value of my services, what they might be willing to pay for a service if it was bundled with something else, if they felt there was anything we could do better or more efficiently, etc.

Single question surveys are great because they're usually a single click impulse item and very easy for the client to answer. You can also be extremely candid with this particular user group because, as we've discussed, they're at the end of the line anyway. That's not to say you want to stop being respectful, just that the communication can be a little more transparent. The naturally combative positioning of buyer/seller is all but removed. This is true for longer form surveys as well. Obviously, a long form survey is a much bigger ask than a single question "click the link" survey but, if you feel you're giving enough value to justify the ask, go for it!

Don't issue surveys just for the sake of them either. Make sure you're getting data and information that helps inform your business processes for the long-term. Do what you can to make the survey process easy on your user base. They'll be willing to help you but you'll alienate folks if you put up barriers that are difficult or tedious, such as forcing them to create a profile before completing your survey form.

Another great source of value that Clients can provide is the ability for you to build solid social proof. You can ask for references, testimonials, case study information and even direct referrals. I wouldn't recommend inundating them with these requests, but just be cognizant of the fact that this is a very reasonable ask, especially when you continue to provide additional value.

Sometimes it's difficult to determine what that additional value may be. My very first "go to" is usually some level of training. The content is typically fast, cheap and easy to make but provides solid value for the recipient and training can be applied to almost any purchase from care and cleaning instructions for products to value amplification and DIY videos for services. The training videos don't even need to relate directly to your exact offering as long as they connect the dots between your offering and the prospect.

Here are a few examples:

- A cabinet manufacturer (who is also a Client of ours) sends out a follow up sequence on the best and most efficient ways to stock a cabinet. They're always a huge hit and get a ton of comments, likes and shares.

- A high-end rug store sends reminders every six months to a year for Clients to rotate their rugs. Once every three to five years they'll send a reminder (as an email and a postcard) to have the rug cleaned. They don't offer cleaning themselves but they include a list of approved vendors.
- A website developer (and friendly competitor of mine) does an excellent job of sending his Clients updates on when Word-Press has updated the CMS and what the implications may be to that update. This sometimes is accompanied by a soft up-sell but, more often, Clients are able to perform the update themselves with the training videos he includes.

Obviously, in some of these cases there's the opportunity for additional business "down the road" but that's not really what we need to be focusing on. Instead, think of your commitment to providing value as a follow through on a promise you have been making, albeit unspoken, since the very beginning of your relationship with these Clients. The follow up value doesn't need to be immense either. If creating training videos or "state of the market" emails is too hard, send out pro-tips, tips & tricks or additional resources from other companies that may be applicable to your user base. Just continue to be of value to your Clients.

Now that we have agreed to be of value for no other reason than its the commitment we made to our Clients in the beginning, let me give you the pretty massive upside. I believe that you will find that your greatest opportunity for long-term growth, specifically in the realm of expanding your services, will be found in these "end of line" Clients. This is true for your own business as well as any business whose digital marketing you manage. When a Client has purchased everything you have to sell, their needs don't magically go away. You simply don't have anything left with which to provide them.

If you're interested in expanding your products/services or looking for additional opportunities for monetization, these are your gold mine Clients. Not only do they already know, like and trust you, they are almost always completely willing to tell you exactly what they need and, in some cases, even what they're willing to pay for it. All you need to do is ask! The key here however is that, as we stated earlier, you don't let this relationship go stale just because you have no way of profiting from it in the short term. Continue to provide value and Clients will continue to look to you as a value provider. Then, when you're ready to expand, you'll have a built in and immediate customer base.

A NOTE ON SELLING YOUR LIST...

THERE IS A VERY LARGE TEMPTATION TO TAKE THE LIST OF CLIENTS WHO HAVE completed your sales cycle and monetize it through third party offers. This is especially true for businesses that truly do have a very clear "end point" with no ability to value optimize or ascend their Clients past a certain point. The next logical option often becomes sending these Clients affiliate offers that may be applicable to them even if such offers are not in your own wheelhouse.

I would be very careful with this approach. I'm not saying that it's never okay to do, just that there is a considerable risk that you could lose credibility and destroy the relationship you've been working so hard to build. I would much rather have a group of people that were simply happy to have done business with me and, if asked, would speak to the value I provided than the same size group of people who have been fractionally monetized through an affiliate model but now feel a little lukewarm about our relationship.

I have seen affiliate offers that worked well, things that truly provided exceptional value to the base we were marketing to. That would be the line in the sand I would ask you to draw: "Is this providing more value to my Clients? Or is this just a way to try and monetize them once last time?" The answer should be clear and make your decision very easy.

APPLICATION SUGGESTIONS

1. Chart the Flow of Value

For those of you who do any level of flow charting or visual mapping of your marketing campaigns and funnels, add an extra visual element the next time you do so. I like to use a separate color and, with an arrow, identify where the value is flowing: from or to the prospect. With the bookended value proposition, the hope would be that you see each "from" flanked by a "to" on either side.

Keep in mind that this isn't always going to be an "every other" distribution. You're more likely to see the following sequence (or something close to it: to—from—to | to—from—to | to—from—to | etc. The reason for this is the fact that the "before value" catalyzes the "from" and the "after value" acts as a bookend. However, it's not always possible for the "after value" to complete a sequence and catalyze the next "from." More often it's better to allow the "after value" to stand alone (which also helps amplify the extra value you're offering) and follow up with an additional value offer later.

2. Don't Be Afraid to Ask

Sometimes, your audience's needs aren't clear or there are additional or ancillary needs that you're not aware of. Make it a habit to ask if there's anything else your prospect would benefit from. This can be done in a myriad of ways. I like to send click-conversion emails on the tail end of a completed value loop that offers a handful of potential future options and ask my prospect to choose the one that appeals to them most. I'd be careful with asking people to fill out forms or surveys, even though the intention is to give them additional value. The draw on their time is still an ask and, therefore, a withdrawal.

Sometimes it can be as easy as having a footnote in each of your outgoing emails that says something to the effect of: "Can you help me help you? My #1 goal is to provide my Customers with the absolute most amount of value possible. Is there something you would benefit from that you think me or my staff could help provide? Please reply to this email and tell me about it!"

3. Spell It Out

While I understand the value of modesty as a virtue in most situations, it's worth toning down and sometimes abandoning completely when it comes to the value you're providing your prospects. First, don't be afraid to make it explicitly clear when you are providing extra or additional value. Sometimes people may mistake your extra deposits as something that's just a part of the process. In other cases, they may think it's too good to be true and assume you're setting them up for an up-sell or bait and switch.

Feel free to be blunt and direct about what you're doing and why you're doing it. Here's an example:

A Client of ours used a home rehab calculator as a lead magnet. A day after the download we sent this email:

> Hi [first-name]!
>
> I hope you are enjoying the rehab calculator you downloaded yesterday. Because I strive to always go above and beyond with everyone I work with, I wanted to share this FREE training video with you on exactly how to use it.
>
> **Please keep this private**, it's only meant for folks that took the time to download the calculator. There are some really great tips in this video and I want them reserved for people like you who are taking the time to actually engage with our content.
>
> Don't worry, there's no sales pitch here. I just wanted to make sure you got the absolute maximum amount of value possible. Everyone who has seen the video so far has loved it, I'm sure you will too. Let me know what you think!

There's nothing subtle about the message above. You're letting them know that the content is super valuable, it's absolutely free and it's only for people who are engaging with your offers. This has the added fringe benefit of encouraging future engagement since they know you're the type of person to follow up with even more value.

4. FAQs Are an Awesome Value Growth Indicator

For every prospect that asks a question, there are probably ten in the background that never pipe up. Use the questions you're getting as an indicator of what might be an opportunity to provide future value. In the example I provided above, our Client was getting a small handful of emails from prospects who downloaded the calculator. It was nothing staggering, just a one-off question here and there about how it's used, advice on their specific situation, questions about how he used it internally, etc.

These questions resulted in the training video we reference above which was a huge hit! The Client received more comments and responses on the follow up training video than he ever did on the original download. The video also helped humanize him in the eyes of his prospects. At first he was just a website that offered a free rehab calculator. After watching the video, his prospects knew who he was, what he looked like, what he sounded like and even got a small taste of his sense of humor.

This doesn't need to be limited to questions you receive about specific offers. Take the general questions you get on a regular basis and find ways to make them a proactive value push that you can put in front of prospects at appropriate stages in the marketing cycle. Because Client purchasing phases are usually similar, you'll start to look like a genius as you anticipate each question they have before they ask it.

5. Recycle

One of the easiest ways to offer up extra value is to reach back into the vault of "stuff" you've been building and bring it back around for a second trip. Every time we retire a lead magnet or a trip wire (for our Clients or ourselves) we look at appropriate opportunities to add it to future funnels as an "after value" follow up. You already know the content is great because you were successfully using it for lead generation. Sneaking it into a funnel for free can only serve to help show you as a constant value provider in the eyes of your prospects.

PRINCIPLE 3
LEARN, APPLY & INNOVATE

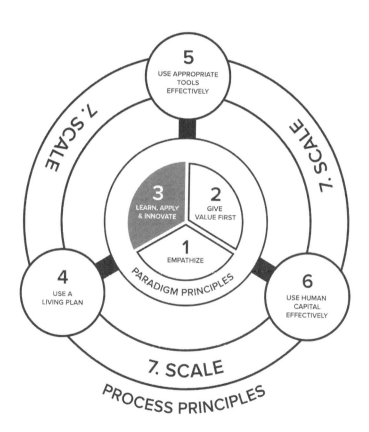

THE THIRD PRINCIPLE IS REALLY A SEQUENCE OF PRINCIPLES FOCUSED ON education. Digital marketing is changing. This will always be true. As fast as you can learn it, and sometimes even faster, digital marketing is expanding into even greater and greater realms of possibility. In fact, trying to keep up would be impossible if you attempt to go it alone. The benefit that you have is that there is absolutely no reason to go it alone. I'll show you what I mean. Let's examine each of the three facets in sequence.

LEARN

YOU HAVE A RESPONSIBILITY TO YOURSELF AND THE PEOPLE YOU SERVE to keep your finger to the pulse. How you do this is completely up to you but you absolutely must commit to doing so. Digital marketing will never be a job; it will always be a lifestyle. If this statement doesn't resonate it might be time to reexamine whether or not this is the correct fit for you. I'm not trying to be dramatic but I am being pragmatic. And pragmatically I can tell you that if you aren't committed and passionate about learning, you are going to be left behind by the majority of digital marketers who are.

Education should be second nature to digital marketers. In one way or another, we are all self-taught. Your presence in this industry speaks to your ability to identify problems and find solutions prior to there being a supposed industry standard. Even now, with as much industry as there is built around digital marketing, it is still the wild west. This is more of a reason to constantly and passionately be looking to remain educated and up to date.

What to Learn

Because there's so much to learn, so many facets to the umbrella that is "digital marketing" and so much noise in general, it is important to cultivate the skill of knowing what to pay attention to and what to discard. The vast majority of us are also technicians of some sort (SEO, Content Writer, Developer, etc.) and as technicians we are used to the granular information being of immense importance. What button to press has been of major concern since we began our journey; when we begin to work on education in other channels of life we might carry that habit with us. As a digital marketer, this is (usually) incorrect.

You don't always need to know how to press buttons. Not that it isn't important, of course it is. It's just not your highest and best use. Think of yourself as a philosophy student and approach your education from that perspective. You're learning what's available, how it's meant to be used, why it should be used and in what contexts, who it's meant to target or serve, how it may be changing, and the impacts it may have on other facets of digital marketing.

The reason I make this distinction is because the educational facet of digital marketing can get extremely daunting otherwise. If you assume that you need to know exactly how every facet and digital marketing proficiency functions, and to a point where you can do it yourself, you're quickly going to go insane. There's no greater mistake than taking a strategist and making him/her a technician. You don't need to know how to run an AdWords campaign but you do need to know when you should run an AdWords campaign, who you should call upon to run it for you and how to manage that person or company.

Don't let yourself get lost in the weeds of education. Make sure that you're building a foundation of knowledge that lets you be a quarterback, not a lawn mower. You're not here to do any one thing. You're here to tie everything together in a way that is strategic and cohesive. Now, if you wear multiple hats and happen to be a technician, don't let me talk you out of staying up to date on your specific vertical. That's not the point of this little dissertation. But, when you're wearing your "digital marketer" hat, realize that you're the general and the general doesn't dig trenches.

The hypocrisy in what I'm saying here is that I have zero ability to define for you what constitutes a trench and what constitutes high level strategy. Everyone's approach, vertical positioning, demographic and business is different. You need to decide for yourself where your focus is best utilized and how to apply it to your specific approach or business model.

When to Learn

As with all things, consistency makes keeping yourself up to date easier on an exponential scale. The same way skipping the gym for a day sets you back a few reps and skipping for a month can set you back a year, making sure you're updated on the industry and its movement is something that needs to be tended to constantly. It becomes so much easier when you work it into your daily routine and regular habits.

Instead of reading the morning news, subscribe to thought leaders and read their daily journals, listen to podcasts instead of the radio on your commute, like and follow thought leaders on social media, commit to reading one white paper a week. Small steps can make huge strides towards staying up to date.

I like to commit to reading one blog a day, one white paper a week and one book per month. It's an aggressive schedule and I'll usually swap things around, change out some videos for a white paper, take a course instead of a book, etc. The basic idea however is still very sound. Something small (10 minutes) each day, something medium sized (one hour) each week and something large (4 hours) per month.

Try to ensure you're getting an adequate amount of variation as well. Committing to only a few thought leaders will limit your ability to expand your horizons past a certain point, even if you're following some of the best in the world. Everyone has blinders in one way or another. Often, some of the best content comes from obscure places. It really pays dividends to spend time investing in finding who is producing the best content, not just who is doing the best job promoting it.

Teaching and Learning

As you're committed to learning, make it a point to begin to teach the core concepts that you learn to others. Learning with the intention to teach forces you to approach the topic with more responsibility. You begin to challenge concepts more because you know that you'll also be challenged. You'll also begin to fact check, test and validate more often so that you don't pass along faux wisdom.

Taking the time to share what you're learning with your employees, vendors, peers and (sometimes) even your Clients, can help position you as a thought leader. I'm also a huge proponent of sprint blogging and believe strongly in its ability to help with retention. Once you've learned a concept up to a point that you feel is adequate, immediately write a blog on the topic. Don't hold back, edit or revise the blog until the very end. Just pretend that your "delete" button doesn't exist and write everything that comes to mind on the topic.

In some cases, you won't even post the blog you've written. In most cases, it'll require a solid once over before being ready for prime time. But in every case, the sprint should give you an excellent refresher to which you can refer later when the topic isn't quite as fresh in your mind. It should also serve to help you retain information longer which, in an interesting turn of cyclical logic, will negate its own reference.

Sources of Education

Thought Leaders

Equally important as what you are learning is who you are learning it from. Where context is key, the source of the information is often one of the most important contextual considerations. I would highly recommend that you spend some time researching and getting to know the thought leaders in your specific vertical. In many cases, these might end up being competitors of yours. That's perfectly fine! Get to know who is producing content in relation to your industry and start making decisions on who you feel provides the most unique value.

There are many reasons to follow several different thought leaders. Sometimes, a person just has an excellent ability to summarize the current state of the industry. These are great folks to follow but be careful in limiting your exposure to them alone because to do so will cause you to miss out on the more "cutting edge" stuff that isn't ready to be included in the "here's what we can all agree upon" category of content.

At the same time, don't fall too hard or fast for the prognosticators of your industry either. They're tons of fun to listen to and usually put you in a creative frame of mind but they're also usually not speaking in very concrete terms. Oftentimes their assertions and assumptions come un-vetted and unsupported, except for maybe some anecdotal evidence. Don't discard them, just temper your intake of their information with proper context applied.

Content Networks

I am a huge fan of content networks. I'm a contributing author to a dozen different networks like Search Engine Journal and Emergent Path. It's worth spending some time on sites like these that aggregate authors and host content from a multitude of perspectives. With that said, be careful of content networks in terms of the amount of trust you place in that content. The authors come to the content networks with varying degrees of credibility and it's important to look into who you are listening to as you engage with the content.

Competitors and Practitioners

In addition to thought leaders and content networks, I would highly recommend subscribing to your competitors, both big and small. In fact, it's usually the little guys that are coming up with the truly game changing marketing tactics. It's a wildly competitive space and for a small company to survive it needs to be nimble and innovative. Quite a few of the best industry disruptor techniques I have seen started with a small agency or solo-consultant.

Learning from Your Clients

As a digital marketer, this is one of the hardest balances to strike. You absolutely need to learn from your Clients to effectively market their product/service. They know infinitely more about what they offer, the value proposition, the Avatar, the pain points, sales cycle, industry, objections and ascension model than you will ever want to know. You need this information to make sure you're not constantly reinventing the wheel or making rookie mistakes. Learning from your Clients should never end and you need to make sure you use them as a resource.

At the same time, it's important to realize that you're being employed because of your unique value and skill set. Sometimes what a Client "knows" isn't always consistent with what we end up finding is the truth. I can't count the number of times I have heard something like "My customers aren't on Facebook" or "People don't search for our service" only to prove the exact opposite to be true. Once again, it falls on you as an expert to know when to follow and when to lead. You're not always going to get it right of course, but recognizing the need for the distinction is half of the battle.

The Decision Maker and the Subject Matter Expert

When you're marketing on behalf of another person or company, sometimes you're placed in a position where the decision maker isn't necessarily the subject matter expert (SME). When you're working with an industry you're unfamiliar with, this can be a difficult distinction to make. I bring it up here because it's applicable to the "learn from your Client" facet of the learning phase. It's important to identify your SME early. It's equally important to make sure your Client understands exactly what an SME is and why having one available to you is necessary.

An office manager isn't a dentist. A CEO probably isn't an engineer. A Director of Marketing isn't a practitioner. That's not to say we should discount these people's opinions, just that we should help to (very early on) make sure they understand that there will be a need to speak to people and experts who are closer to the product, service or customer than they may be. Your decision maker will always have the final say, but try to make sure that it's not the only say. I can't count the number of times a CMO made an assertion and was later shocked to find his sales staff in complete disagreement with his view.

It's your job to sniff out the proper source of information and act from that appropriate vantage point. Sometimes this means having difficult conversations. You have the responsibility to protect your Client from his or herself and make sure you're getting the absolute best information available. Otherwise you're putting the Client at a massive disadvantage and all but ensuring that you'll end up sharing in the blame for a failed or inadequate campaign.

Sometimes you're learning from the Client and sometimes you're just learning about the Client. Their beliefs about their business can be just as shortsighted as anyone else's. We all have our blind spots; you are being placed in the interesting position of having to recognize those blind spots in others. This is much easier said than done. I have found the easiest way to approach this is to simply challenge assumptions. Always ask "why?" Get to the root of core beliefs and you'll start to see where and how they were formed. In some cases, you'll find that they're well founded and supported by very real data and experience. Other times you'll find that something happened one time that catalyzed an entire belief system.

Marketing Is Learning

That last facet of learning might be the most important. Make it a point to learn from your own initiatives and campaigns. All too often we become so obsessed with making something work that we glaze over the learning lessons that are housed within our failures. You will often hear that over 80% of all online ads fail. This means that as digital marketers we need to embrace the "fail early and fail often" mantra. This does not mean failure for the sake of it obviously but instead embracing the knowledge that failure will happen. If we ignore it we'll only end up wasting time and money.

However, when failure does happen we should always reflect on the why. Spend some time with it. Sometimes, learning what doesn't work is equally as important as learning what does. I'm not asking you to apply meaning where there is none or to play the "correlation must be causation" game that we all tend to get into trouble with. I'm simply saying you shouldn't leave failure unexamined. If a campaign doesn't work, try to determine why. Look for the point of failure and examine it. At a minimum, it might help point you in the right direction and keep you from repeating the mistake.

In the same way we should learn from our failures, we should also learn from our successes. While this sounds like it should go without saying, all too often we see marketers running the same patterns even after identifying what can and should work. There's very little excuse for repeating a mistake. Sometimes we don't realize that the mistakes we're making are baked into our processes. If you continue to make the same type of correction or find success in the same direction of change, maybe it's time to modify your process or starting point.

APPLY

THERE'S A REASON THIS IS A THREE-PART PRINCIPLE. THESE PARTS CAN'T STAND alone. Learning for the sake of learning might be fulfilling and have its own merit in a world where the expansion of the mind is a virtue unto itself. Sadly, that's not the case in the realm of digital marketing. In digital marketing, learning without application yields the same amount of value as cloud watching or a bracketed thumb war competition.

If you're going to learn you need to apply what you learn, but you also need to have a system for said application. You can't come into the office each morning screaming about the latest and greatest and demanding that all campaigns be rebuilt, I have tried and it doesn't work. The best way to apply new learning to existing processes is by building a process for it. I know, mind blowing, right?

Every month, my entire staff and I participate in a half-day long meeting we have appropriately named "monthly plan"—you know, because we're creative types. Monthly plan covers quite a few points of discussion but one of the most prominent is new ideas. Everyone is tasked with taking ownership of their specific vertical and coming to the meeting with ideas as to how we might change and improve on our current processes. After discussing the implications of each suggested improvement, we identify the action items tethered to the improvements we're interested in pursuing.

Typically, we identify one campaign (existing or upcoming) that will be an effective test for the new approach. The vast majority of the time it is something we're already doing internally. However, we have used Client campaigns in the past as well. As we roll out a new approach for a Client campaign, we're very clear as to what we're proposing and why, and always note any potential risks involved. The campaign is monitored, measured and then reviewed at the next monthly plan. If we like the results, we discuss how to roll it out to other campaigns. Sometimes we decide to conduct a few more tests and sometimes we abandon it entirely.

I'm not saying our process is the best process. You might want to review new ideas quarterly or weekly. Just make sure that you're not making knee jerk decisions because you were impassioned by a really well written blog or watched a 20-minute video from some hopped-up guru and decided to rewrite your entire business model. Regardless of how you decide to approach change, make sure that change is a part of your approach. You can't stay the same in this business and, if you do, it's a recipe for no longer being in business.

Romantics Make Bad Digital Marketers

There's a very real danger in getting attached to a specific verti-cal, process or network. When you've gotten good at something it's easy to become attached to it, even take a little ownership over it. As an SEO, I will forever love Google. I'll sing its praises and lament the day it's no longer the Lord of the internet. Because I know this about myself, I'm very cautious in discarding other options in lieu of sticking with my tried and true Google Machine. Not only am I "good at it," I built my entire business on it.

As a PPC company, we've been Google focused for half a dec-ade. When Facebook became a viable second option it was ex-tremely easy for us to discard it as fancy banner advertising. Many of my competitors are still standing on that platform, insistent upon the fact that Facebook is "push marketing" and not worthy of inclusion in an inbound marketing paradigm. As this was going on almost half of my PPC business became Facebook (at the time of this writing) and I anticipate that number multiplying in the months and years to come.

I don't like Facebook. I think the ad delivery mechanism is clunky, ad builder is limiting and the lead generation tools are laughable (csv download Facebook, really?) But it works. For some Clients, it works phenomenally well, better than Google ever could. If I wanted to stay romantic about my relationship with Google, I'd be missing out on one of the biggest potential verticals available to my agency at the moment.

For that matter, look at Bing. If I dislike Facebook, I hate Bing. It's a ridiculous tool that continues to work at a stated goal of only be-ing second best. Bing innovates nothing and provides zero value, surviving only on building strong strategic relationships with third party networks that force users to pass through Bing's ecosystem. A brilliant move on Microsoft's part but frustratingly limiting when you're a fan of a Bing partner. With all of that said, we still continue to test Bing with every single new PPC and SEO Client. Why? Be-cause Bing has a user base that, however small, has been proven to be effectively monetized in the right contexts.

Google may fail one day. It may go the way of Netscape and be relegated to nothing more than a cautionary tale about which busi-ness majors are forced to write. Rome fell to Germanic tribes. I'm not equipped to accurately predict the next big thing. I don't know that anyone is. The best thing we can do as digital marketers is to make sure that our livelihoods aren't built on the backs of any single entity or strategy.

People are all too fond of telling us what is dead. SEO is dead. Email marketing is dead. Traditional marketing is dead. In a world that is fond of killing that which continues to breathe, just make sure you're able to see the forest through the picket signs disguised as trees. Don't abandon something because someone tells you it may not work in the future. At the same time, don't let what's working now distract you from what may work tomorrow.

Plausible Deniability

I feel that a large segment of my peers don't like to learn because they're afraid that it will force their hand. If they don't learn anything new, they maintain the moral high ground in continuing to do it the way that they are doing it. While this may not be a conscious decision, I think it's a firmly rooted subconscious belief inhibits good digital marketers from becoming great digital marketers.

There is no plausible deniability in our field. Learning is a prerequisite. You can't bury your head in the sand and keep on keeping on. There may be industries where this approach is excusable and maybe even preferable but ours isn't one of them. Just because you don't know a certain way is the better way doesn't mean that it isn't the better way. You have a responsibility to yourself, your staff and your Clients to force growth.

There is no excuse for ignorance. If you're afraid that your business model is antiquated, then you should be the very first person to tear down the veil and work to correct the problem. What I find most interesting is that, far more often than not, this is an excellent opportunity disguised as a problem. You now have the ability to proactively approach every Client you have with a feasible up-sell that'll do nothing but cement you as a thought leader in their eyes.

It takes a lot of courage to self-correct. When the ship starts to sink, you'll lose Clients faster than you ever thought possible. The only way to mitigate this risk is to guide the ship to safe harbor and help transition everyone to a more appropriate vessel for transport.

INNOVATE

As with the first two facets of this multi-part principle, innovation cannot stand alone. Learning and the application of what you're learning is an integral part of the entire process. But to be effective digital marketers we need to strive for even more. We need to be a part of the digital vanguard. A digital marketer is a scientist, not an order taker. The highest version of this principle is found through innovation.

Innovate and experiment

There's no right way to perform digital marketing. If you're treating your campaigns like they're a static system of steps that are just meant to be built, implemented and monitored, you're not providing much more value than a machine. While processes and best practices are wildly important, it's important not to relegate ourselves to process alone.

Even though innovation and experimentation may constitute a fraction of the work we're performing, it might be the most important part of our journey. Quantity of time spent doesn't always dictate quality in the expenditure. You might spend 5% of your time experimenting and yet find that it yields 90% of your growth and unique value when you start to identify new and innovative approaches.

Every Client you serve is an opportunity for growth that could benefit both you and your Client. I don't believe that you should be taking wild stabs at brand new strategic initiatives. Instead, I think you should stick with the tried and true to prove value but, with the last 5% to 10% of the campaign, work to innovate new and strategic methods for greater performance.

Always be testing

The easiest way to approach constant innovation is to always be testing. There's no reason not to run continuous AB and split tests. Run tests until the variations get granular or until the results stop yielding a clear winner. Once you've reached that point, start over with a different set of variables. You can never run out of things to split test. From ad copy, page copy, CTA, images, landing page format, colors, pricing, subject lines, font and font sizes, there's a nearly limitless number of assumptions you're making on an ongoing basis that should be tested to tedium.

If you're driving traffic to a property you are wasting an opportunity by not split testing that property in some way. You don't need to get drastic with your tests. In fact, I have found it's much better to test simple, easily identifiable differences then large, contrasting things that make the "why" difficult to determine. When you're testing, make sure you're only testing one variable or you could run into a scenario of interdependent differences. Otherwise, make it a habit to always split test any single facet of a marketing campaign.

How to Fail Good and Succeed Better

If you're a digital marketer, fear of failure can't be a thing. Digital marketing **is** failing until you succeed. The very nature of our business requires us to constantly fail as we make assumptions and educated guesses as to what might work. The key to failing for a living is to make sure you're doing so in a systematic fashion and within the confines of well-mitigated risks. Build your program in a way that can absorb failure as part of the system. This will help you find success quickly and repeatedly and stay sane while you're doing it.

The core process of failing good (the bad grammar is meant to be ironic incidentally) is as follows:

- Make an assumption
- Define the control group
- Build the test environment and select the variables
- Run and monitor the test
- Gather and evaluate data
- Determine results
- Identify successes and failures
- Repeat

The process outlined above can be modified and adjusted to suit your business model or the specific vertical you're working with at the time. The point is that you have a process for testing your assumptions and that you're not just throwing spaghetti against the wall. This also makes it exceedingly important that you educate your Client as to what you're doing and why.

Selling digital marketing services is dangerous for this very reason. It's hard to communicate competence and experience and at the same time properly manage expectations around the fact that your Client is really just paying you to make their mistakes for them. The best way to do this is to take a deep dive into what digital marketing truly is and why every single Client (even Clients in the same industry) are so very different.

If you glaze over your processes with empty promises, you're going to find yourself in a world of hurt. However, if you explain your processes to Clients, and illustrate the value in what you provide, you'll be met with understanding and massive amounts of help when it comes to building and testing assumptions. Importantly, the Clients you lose (because you will lose Clients when you're unwilling to make unrealistic promises) are Clients that you never ever wanted in the first place. I promise.

When you're building these tests, alongside your Client or on your own, it's important that you don't fall victim or prey to analysis paralysis. This is a byproduct of the fear of failure that we have already agreed can't be a thing. You need to destroy any feelings that live in this realm immediately and with a vengeance. You need to make a decision and then own the results. When you fail, it's important that you learn from that failure and work not to make the same mistake twice.

Here's what's interesting about all this mistake making and data gathering. Sometimes you find out what works but can't find out why it works. It's a dangerous place to be, but it happens. My opinion is: run with it. As long as you're transparent with your Client about what you're doing and why, there's no reason not to capitalize on success just because you don't understand it. Try. Try very hard to get to the bottom of what the catalyst to success was. Otherwise you won't be able to learn from it. But if you never get to a point where you understand exactly what made you succeed that's okay, succeed anyway.

You Can't Be Afraid of Failure but You Can't Not Let It Hurt Either

This is where the conversation gets very real: you don't always make the jump. Sometimes you burn a Client's patience faster than you make progress on the campaign. Sometimes you work tirelessly attempting to find the magic formula to lead production (or funnel conversion or retention or whatever) and just can't connect the dots. It happens. Hopefully not often, but it happens to the absolute best of us for a multitude of reasons that are far too numerous to name...

- The Client's product isn't viable in the market
- The market is too small
- You're using the wrong methods or mechanisms
- The spend was too low
- The price point too high
- The turnaround time was too short
- The sun didn't shine brightly enough that day

And sometimes you have no idea why you can't make it work. It's not any harder than half a dozen other campaigns that you completely knocked out of the park but, for whatever reason, it won't fly. I think I'm supposed to tell you not to let these eat you up inside but, honestly, I don't think that's correct either. I think they should burn. The hurt should be very real and very personal.

I never take a Client if I don't believe there's at least a reasonable possibility of success. And I never run a campaign without leaving every ounce of myself out on the field. If you're a good digital marketer, then what I'm saying should resonate with you. Put this book down right this very instant, Google Al Pacino's monologue in "Any Given Sunday" and pretend that he's talking about digital marketing and not football. You should be balled up in the fetal position wailing uncontrollably like a toddler who just saw Elmo murdered in a drive-by.

I need you to take this seriously. This is important. Oftentimes we're a business's last and only shot at seeing success or the only thing keeping them from experiencing miserable failure. While I never advocate gambling with someone else's last buck, I don't think any amount of money that a small business shells out is a small amount of money. There's a sacred trust here and that trust needs to be quantified by many multiples based solely on the fact that we are professional mistake makers.

What I'm trying to say is this: When failure is par for the course, it's vital that the player is someone who is going to see the game through to the very end and beyond. The stakes are too high and the costs too great to let a bunch of looky-loos and tourists play on the field. What we do is real and its impact is long-lasting. I have a personal reputation to protect, of course, but I also have an industry reputation to uphold—we all do.

119

APPLICATION SUGGESTIONS

1. 30 Minutes a Day

Everyone has 30 minutes in the day that they can afford to allocate more effectively. Find a block of time that you can commit to the third principle. There's simply no alternative for constant and focused attention to learning. If you can build a daily routine, you'll start to find that you look forward to it. If you really love digital marketing, then you'll start to get excited about these little mental excursions. And if you don't really love digital marketing, please find something that you do love and go do that! You can make more money with less headache at so many other things.

I would caution you against getting overly ambitious with this allocation of time. If you have no problem spending more than 30 minutes a day on this task then, by all means, do so. However, after about a month it can lose its honeymoon phase appeal at which point it's just more important that you stick to it than spend excessive amounts of time on it. I have found that 30 minutes is enough time to identify a single high value piece of content, imbibe it and then take a few notes on my immediate impressions or things on which I'd like to do follow up research in subsequent days.

I also try to take notes on things I find to be immediately actionable. While this isn't always practical, I do like to avoid reading for the sake of reading. There's nothing wrong with reading for pleasure—I do that too—but this particular exercise is meant to identify thoughts, processes and ideas that you can introduce into your business to help spur your growth. For that reason, I keep a Google doc where I jot down ideas I come across that I may want to revisit as potential action items.

2. Read and Write

I like to toggle my daily learning time (which averages 30 to 45 minutes) between reading and writing. If I read yesterday, then I'll write today. I don't necessarily have to write about what I learned yesterday, but it's not uncommon for that to be the topic I find most available to me. I don't have a set structure for learning. I like to allow myself the flexibility to breathe and explore. If you would prefer watching videos or listening to podcasts, you will obviously adjust the learning approach to whatever suits your personal style of information intake most effectively.

Writing helps me to retain information but it also helps me explore thoughts and ideas. It's not uncommon at all for something I write to be completely discarded, but I almost always find value in the exercise of examining a new idea or an old concept in a new way. I usually aim to write about 1,000 words or as close as I can get before I run out of time. This target is ambitious for a reason; if I'm writing on a topic and I'm forced to stretch the lengths of what the topic might deserve, I find myself examining it from angles from which I normally wouldn't approach it.

Writing doesn't necessarily need to be the creation outlet you choose. It just happens to be the one that works best for me. If you would rather create a daily video I'm sure that would accomplish much the same thing. I have a colleague who uses a mind mapping software and spends time mind mapping ideas and concepts. The mind maps can often become easily actionable since they're already broken down into a form that can transition into a process.

Regardless of how you choose to create, I would caution you against reading (or watching or listening) alone. Simply performing data intake without finding a way to utilize what you're learning, even if it's only for yourself, tends to limit your ability to make that information actionable. If you're going to apply the things you learn, the very first step is to examine them from a more personal perspective. Reading something is great but writing about it allows you to contextualize it according to your own specific situation which makes the opportunity to find areas of specific application much easier and far more likely to occur.

3. Go outside Your Industry

I like to subscribe to authors that I find myself revisiting often, regardless of their vertical. Nate Silver (the snarky statistician) is an excellent example of a content creator that has nothing to do with digital marketing and yet provides me with so much in the way of thought ammunition. The content Nate produces tends to center around identifying patterns in data, something that I can apply directly to my own practice.

This is true for a wide variety of content networks. I find value in reading about new technology, psychology, human behavior, statistics and even politics and popular culture. In fact, some of my most trafficked blog articles over the years have been things that I have written after newsjacking an article and finding a way to make recent news analogous to digital marketing.

I also find that, in terms of innovation, it can be easier to think outside of the box when you are constantly filling yourself up with information from directly within the box. This doesn't mean that we should seek out obscure content for the sake of obscurity but, instead, that there might be innovation and accelerated thought patterns in other industries that we can mirror in our own. For example, I have learned quite a bit about funnel marketing from reading and listening to seasoned real estate investors. Real estate is a saturated industry which forces constant innovation. However, it's not exceptionally sophisticated in the digital sense, so most of the real estate marketing tactics are to which I refer are analog.

The things these investors do on an analog level can be easily translated to the digital realm. For example, I learned from one very popular investor's podcast that when he deploys "bandit signs" (those ugly little signs you see staked to the ground at stop lights that say "I want to buy your house for cash") he has found that ugly, hand written signs perform better than professional, printed signs. Anecdotally, he assumed it's because people would prefer to try and sell their house to someone they think might be less sophisticated and therefore, more likely to make a mistake.

I tested this same approach with some of the landing pages for my real estate investment Client and was shocked to see the exact same concept applied. The less sophisticated landing pages that looked like they were pulled together by someone who didn't really know web design actually performed better than our super flashy landing pages that I had my designer build.

Every industry on the planet has something just like this to offer. It's up to you to sniff it out.

PROCESS PRINCIPLES OVERVIEW

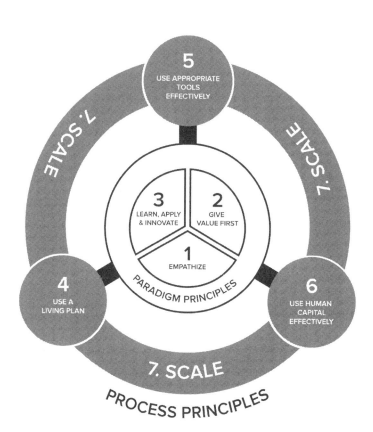

THE PROCESS PRINCIPLES ARE THE "HOW." THESE PRINCIPLES ARE:

- Use a living plan
- Use appropriate tools effectively
- Use human capital effectively
- Scale

They are the core principles that guide the way we take action on our digital marketing initiatives. Following process principles ensures that we put strategy ahead of tactics. Keep in mind that the process principles are built on top of the paradigm principles. Where the paradigm principles can stand alone, the process principles (where applicable) rely on the paradigm principles to guide their execution.

The process principles should directly impact the approach you take in your day to day digital marketing efforts. You will more than likely find that you are already following quite a few of these principles naturally. Given that these are the logical manifestation of a natural order, it would not be surprising to find that you are following all or almost all of them. I believe the added layer of value that I have been able to apply is my specific approach to the process principles.

While I find these principles to be axiomatic, the way everyone goes about implementing the principles is going to be wildly different and will vary according to target vertical, typical campaign size, core proficiencies, etc. Make sure to make these process principles your own. Modify the recommended approaches in order that they more effectively apply to your unique business.

It's extremely important, when dealing with process principles, that the emphasis not be on the specific manner of execution. The idea and core focus of the principles needs to be honored in order to derive maximum benefit from them. The implementation presented here is a matter of opinion. It can be used in its entirety, modified or even completely discarded. As long as you're able to stay true to the principle, the manner in which that principle is integrated into your process is completely up to you.

The principles will ultimately be far more effective once you've taken ownership of them. Following them as though they're outside rules acting upon you as an external force will limit their efficacy. Building them into the psyche of your business, training your staff, vendors and even Clients on them, will ensure that they find ways to permeate facets of your campaign and activity that you wouldn't otherwise have realized was even possible.

PRINCIPLE 4
USE A LIVING PLAN

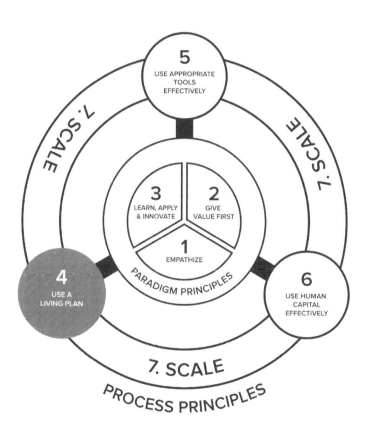

WHEN WAS THE LAST TIME YOU LOOKED AT YOUR MARKETING PLAN? IF YOU have multiple Clients, when was the last time you looked at a Client's marketing plan? Do you even have a marketing plan in place?

A plan is something you follow. It should be an ongoing reference guide for everything you do. The point of a "living plan" is to build something that is at the center of all your marketing initiatives, something that is updated and referenced often and something to which everyone involved has access.

The marketing plan should be where needle-mover tasks are assigned, key performance indicators are tracked, rocks are set, major decisions are documented and success is realized.

In order for a plan to be "living" you need it to reside somewhere that is accessible. I would recommend putting your living plans in a cloud tool. We use Google Spreadsheet. We'll talk more about this in subsequent sections.

PLAN, REVIEW, DOCUMENT, REPEAT

AS WE DISCUSSED IN PRINCIPLE 3, PEOPLE ARE PAYING YOU TO MAKE THEIR mistakes for them. That means that you have a responsibility to document those mistakes. Hopefully you'll also document a success or two along the way. A lot of digital marketing mavericks feel that planning is wasted time and just gets in the way—that's because they're not doing it right.

I have no issues with agile project management methodologies. I see their value and am a huge proponent of their use. However, a lot of project managers have decided that "agile" really means "No planning at all! Let's just fly by the seat of our pants and see what happens." An agile approach still needs to be documented and followed.

The principle being presented here isn't simply to use a plan; the principle is to use a *living* plan. The folks who believe that plans don't work are the folks that made a plan on day 1, put it in the drawer and never looked at it again. For the plan to work for you, you have to work the plan. Oh, clichés hurt! They hurt more when they're true. The key to working a plan is to make it a functional document that you review on a regular basis and utilize to document your progress.

A living plan is organic and ever-changing. Just because you made a plan doesn't mean you need to stick to it! In fact, I firmly believe that changing the plan should be part of the plan. Build in regular intervals for review and to discuss potential adjustments. Part of the reason that people abandon plans so quickly is because of the rigidity that's built into them.

At the same time, a living plan will help ensure that you aren't changing too much too often. As dangerous as it is to get stubbornly committed to a single course of action, it's equally dangerous to change with every blow of the wind. A good living plan will outline planned intervals for review and course correction. Sticking to these intervals will ensure that certain approaches are given a fair work out time to prove success prior to any knee jerk reaction being given the opportunity to throw them off course.

In the business of digital marketing it's easy to get distracted. It's easy to chase dreams, momentary wins, and competitors. It's easy to overreact to a bad report or over correct when a Client complains or offers up an objection. The living plan will help ensure that this isn't quite as big a temptation. It'll help keep everyone honest and re-mind you, your staff, your vendors and your Clients where you're heading and how you've decided to get there.

COMPONENTS OF A LIVING PLAN

No MATTER HOW YOU HOUSE IT, THE MARKETING PLAN NEEDS TO BE FUNC-tional and organic. Putting a scope of work on a piece of paper doesn't do anyone any good if it doesn't result in an actionable plan. The goals of the plan need to be tracked on an ongoing basis to en-sure you're climbing a ladder that is propped up against the correct wall.

Your living plan needs to be built around your business. Because digital marketing is so multifaceted, it would be impossible for me to present the "right way" to build or utilize a living plan. However, in order to provide you with as much value as I can, I wouldn't feel comfortable simply presenting the principle in generic terms. Instead, I have decided to share the living plan that my agency uses internally.

I will use this living plan as an example and explain each of the core components. Please keep in mind that this living plan is built around my agency and structured to serve our purposes. You will need to revise the plan in order to suit your specific agency needs. For example, my agency puts a strong focus and emphasis on content creation which you will see reflected in our living plan. If your agency is focused more on paid ad management, you might do the same thing with core ad campaigns.

You can access an abbreviated version of our living plan here: kasim.me/living-plan

IMPORTANT NOTE:

I didn't want to turn this book into some affiliate pitch fest. There's nothing wrong with affiliate marketing but it obviously kills any impartiality the author may have been able to claim. With that said, when you review our living plan you will see a substantial amount of content and concepts have been taken from DigitalMarketer.com.

I'm a huge fan of Digital Marketer. My agency is a Digital Marketer Certified Partner and every member of my staff is required to go through Digital Marketer training. I drank the kool-aid and still wear the t-shirt.

The entire "Living Plan" chapter would have been compromised if I didn't offer an example of a living plan and the best example I have relies heavily on educational concepts that I took from Digital Marketer.

Here is a breakdown of the core components of our living plan:

- Campaign abstract
    - Marketing mission statement
    - Scope of work
    - S.M.A.R.T. Digital Marketing Goals
    - Key Performance Indicators

- Client Research
  - Company story (soul)
  - SWOT analysis
  - Product/market fit
  - Statement of value
  - Explanation of product/service
  - Competitive analysis
  - Industry analysis
- Avatar(s)
- Regular management
  - Rocks
  - Milestones
  - Tasks
- Reports

Let's take a look at each of these components in greater details.

Campaign Abstract

Marketing Mission Statement

The marketing mission statement is the simple narrative. In very plain English, state what it is that you're setting out to accomplish. The mission statement should be referenced often and used as the primary barometer when discussing major strategic changes or additions.

If you ever find yourself in a position where what you're doing (the tasks you're performing) no longer serves the marketing mission statement, treat it as an immediate and urgent red flag and indication that something needs to change.

When a Client wants to change direction, add a new initiative, or involve a new partner, it's important to refer them to your marketing mission statement and challenge the new inclusion against the original statement of purpose.

Often, our day to day actions are inconsistent with the goal toward which we are reaching. For example, if the primary purpose for your marketing campaign is to develop high quality leads it may not be the best allocation of time or resources to embark on brand development campaigns.

The mission statement can also be used as a "best fit" litmus test. If you're looking at a collection of potential initiatives, use the mission statement to determine which approach is holistically the best fit or the most consistent with your mission statement.

Sometimes we experience a change that is drastic enough to require that we change the mission statement. The Client's needs may change, the market may change, information we earn through the campaign may negate the original mission. Regardless of how or why it happens, if you retire your mission statement you'll probably need to build a new marketing plan.

Scope of Work

A clearly defined scope of work will give you the opportunity to reference exactly what you're being paid for. This is a summary of the services you are providing. Think of this as the "Cliff's Notes" to the contract between you and your Client. I like including the scope of work in the living plan because it ensures that it is always visible for you, your staff, your vendors and your Clients.

If you have been a digital marketer for longer than seventeen minutes then you have experienced a project's ability to creep. You start off providing AdWords management and suddenly find yourself building and optimizing an entire sales funnel. There's absolutely nothing wrong with this expansion of services, it means you're doing your job! You just want to make sure that the agreed upon scope is clearly and concisely available for constant reference. Doing so puts you in a better position to ascend Clients when the time comes.

Interestingly, you and your staff are probably as guilty of scope creep as your Clients are. Digital marketing is fun! It is an easy thing to get excited about, especially when a campaign starts to really work. What I have often found is that my team ends up adding on additional services as a campaign requires it without realizing that we should be billing for the added time.

S.M.A.R.T. Digital Marketing Goals

The primary goals for the marketing campaign need to be reviewed regularly. These goals should be reported against and, where possible, broken up into smaller goals to gauge velocity and identify your "rocks" and milestones.

Remember to always utilize SMART goals: Specific, Measurable, Actionable, Realistic and Time based. Goals that can't be quantified or acted on are not goals, they are wishful thinking. "We want to make more money" isn't a goal. "We want to make $100,000 in additional monthly recurring revenue by the end of this fiscal year" is a SMART goal.

Ideally, no marketing campaign should have more than three goals—three or less is preferable. If you try to do too many things, they're all going to fail. Oftentimes, as digital marketers, we fall into a trap of trying to prove our value by a large showing of deliverable items. This can include goals and profit benchmarks, where we justify the amount we're charging in proportion to the amount of promises we make. This is a mistake.

As you learn to charge what you're worth, that lesson needs to be accompanied by the fact that part of the value you bring to the table is assisting the Client in defining focused initiatives and moving toward them. A bigger price tag might mean bigger goals but it doesn't (and shouldn't) mean more of them.

Your reporting and key performance indicators (which we'll talk more about later in this section) should be built around your core goals. This keeps the campaign honest and helps to avoid the temptation of only reporting on the metrics that make the campaign look successful, something of which far too many digital marketers are guilty.

Reporting against defined goals will also help protect you from the shiny object disease that so many of our Clients possess. If you're working with small and medium sized businesses, then you're working with Entrepreneurs, and Entrepreneurs are notorious for their willingness to take chances and make leaps of faith. In many cases, it's what makes them successful!

Regardless of the potential merit in an Entrepreneur's willingness to pivot, you need to make sure you're positioned to remind the decision maker as to what your stated purpose is and has been since the campaign began. Reporting against specific goals helps drive this point home consistently. That way, if a change is requested (or demanded) you'll be well-positioned from the vantage point of having managed appropriate expectations.

Key Performance Indicators

Your key performance indicators (KPIs) are the data points you're going to use to measure the success of your marketing campaign. The key performance indicators are typically a measurement of the primary campaign goals. In some cases you may find that you only have one key performance indicator. That's perfectly acceptable. If the primary goal of the campaign is to generate a certain number of leads then the KPI would be the number of leads generated this month.

As marketers, we often fall into the "more data is better data" trap, especially when we're in a position where we're proving our worth to a Client. We want to produce as much information as possible to support the fact that we are working diligently on their campaign. While this reporting has a place, that place is not in our living plan.

Key performance indicators exist to soften the "noise" of the millions of data points that are available to us as digital marketers. They help to simplify the tracking of our digital marketing initiatives and boil them down to a handful of very straightforward metrics. The KPIs exist as a constant measurement of the primary purpose of the campaign's existence.

The key performance indicators should be decided upon alongside the Client or key decision maker. The Client should be involved in the discussions, development and final decision as to what the KPIs are, how to quantify them and how a specific KPI will be measured. Even if everyone agrees on a KPI, the way that data point is collected, measured and reported on could become a point of contention. Make sure you've clearly outlined how KPIs will be measured in order to mitigate that risk. Here are some examples:

- KPI: Total number of leads
  - What qualifies as a lead?
  - What types of information need to be collected for a prospect to be considered a lead?
  - Is there a lead quality threshold that should be met? If so, how is that measured? What is the process for reporting the lead from the sales team back to the marketing team?
- KPI: Organic website traffic
  - What are the most valuable key phrases in terms of user intention?
  - What are the most important pages and on-site resources to drive traffic to?
  - Are there any referral sources that should be excluded?
  - Are there any behavioral identifiers that should be filtered out?

- KPI: Total cost per acquisition (CPA) of a new customer
  - What is the equation we should use to reach this number? Are we calculating the CPA based off the ad spend alone or should the agency fee be included? Should we factor in foundational costs like our Customer Relationship Management (CRM) and various marketing tools? If so, how should they be split between new Clients?
  - Can we count referrals from Customers who originally came from digital marketing efforts?
    - NOTE: this is something I'm extremely passionate about. When you're working with Clients, make sure to make the case that the lifetime value of a customer isn't limited to what they spend with the company. It extends to anyone they refer as well. This is part of the value that should be quantified when you're reporting on the success of a digital marketing campaign.

These are three examples of hundreds, if not thousands, of possibilities. It all depends on what the Client's primary goals are. KPIs can be focused on customer retention, website bounce rate, brand mentions on twitter, new followers on snapchat, email open & click through rates, etc. Whatever the KPI is, just make sure that you're equipped to measure it in a way that is consistent with your decision maker's expectations.

Because digital marketing is so dynamic, it's easy for us to be derailed by ancillary or unseen successes. Oftentimes our successes can be as much of a danger as our failures; this is especially true if the success you're experiencing doesn't drive the core business goal. The danger is that we get tempted to start working a data point that isn't driving one of our core goals.

Using key performance indicators as a constant guide will help ensure that the core goals are constantly top of mind. They also help to act as an internal thermometer that can signal when a core goal is no longer as important and needs to be changed. If the Client begins losing interest in the KPIs that are associated with a goal, that's a red flag that the goal you are driving toward is no longer worthy of the primary attentions of your campaign.

Key performance indicators will also help protect you in a world where managing expectations is one of the most valuable skills a digital marketer can have. I've been in situations where a Client has

135

called me absolutely irate that they aren't able to find their website when they perform a google search for their core key phrases. The fact that they chose to pass on our search engine optimization services did nothing to deter them from blowing up.

Building KPIs alongside your Client (or manager or decision maker) and keeping them "top of mind" with every report will help reinforce the goals toward which the campaign is driving. They also help to mitigate risk and appease Clients who suffer from shiny object disease by reminding them what the purpose of the campaign is and should remain.

There's an old adage that I have printed out and taped above my desk: "That which is measured is managed." If you don't build for and report against a small set of wildly important key metrics, you are asking for a digital marketing plan that is disjointed and inconsistent. It's not that you won't be successful. In fact you might experience more tangential successes if you're given the opportunity to roam freely across the broad landscape of digital marketing possibilities. But those successes aren't what you have been hired for. When the track ball meets the mouse pad, tangential successes aren't the purpose of the campaign.

Client Research

It's important to include Client research in the living plan so the project manager, team members, vendors and even the Client can refer to it throughout the phases of marketing. This acts as a reminder as to why you made certain decisions. It also enables you to bring on new resources throughout the campaign and immediately catch them up on who the Client is.

A lot of what we do as digital marketers is educated guesswork, especially in the very beginning of a Client's campaign. We gather the information we are able to and then utilize that data to make assumptions. These assumptions will change over the course of the marketing campaign.

If you aren't tracking your original assumptions, then you aren't paying attention to those changes. The changes in your assumptions are marked progress in the digital marketing campaign. Not only can they be utilized to illustrate value in terms of what you are learning, they are also important reference points to look back on when you revisit previous actions.

We might not always remember why we decided on a specific course of action. Not having the "why" in front of us makes it easier for us to justify impetuous changes or adjustments. Keeping our research at the forefront of our marketing plan helps to act as a gentle reminder of why we chose the approaches we took.

The first phase of your research should be based around your Client. You need to be trained as though you are the newest member of their executive sales staff. Find out how they operate, what their corporate culture is and what their value system looks like. The Client onboarding piece is an important part of your plugging into the Client's business.

One of the most important discussions in the onboarding of a new Client is the business's long-term goals. By this, I don't mean their goals in relation to digital marketing, I mean their overarching goals in general. If you're going to be a true Client advocate, you want to make sure you're driving your initiatives in the same direction as their primary goals.

For example, a business which wants to be positioned for acquisition will require different marketing approaches from a business looking to expand into new geographies. Digital marketing should work in tandem with the business goals. Often it is far more tempting to simply point your muzzle at the opportunities that appear to be the lowest hanging fruit.

I have outlined the components that we use for the "Client" section within our living plan. Again, please keep in mind that these are built around serving our model, which is extremely content focused. You will need to add/edit/delete according to your model and the services you provide.

Company Story (Soul)

This is huge. Understanding who the company is, where they came from and where they are going is an absolute necessity for our team. Because we create content on behalf of the Client, we need to be able to speak with their voice. Our ability to capture their perspective is often the most important factor in how successful our campaigns are.

The type of information available and the manner in which it is presented will change with each company. It isn't our job to try to fit their story into our template. Instead, we want to allow this to be a very malleable section of the living plan; we focus on what the Client thinks is important.

The company story is exceptionally helpful then we bring in new resources to assist with the campaign. We may end up with a new hire that we bring in to assist, a change in staff, or even an added service that requires roping in a new vendor or outside resource. In each case we have the ability to quickly and easily catch our new resource up on who the Client is.

SWOT Analysis

SWOT is an acronym that stands for Strengths, Weaknesses, Opportunities, Threats. You see this often in business plans and for good reason. This is meant to be a snapshot of the potentially catalytic elements an organization is currently facing, both positive and negative.

Understanding a business's strengths allows you the opportunity to speak to those strengths and capitalize on their market position. It even allows you to get bullish in your marketing efforts since you know that they're well positioned in a certain area.

In the exact same way that understanding strengths will enable you to position yourself for success, understanding weaknesses will allow you to mitigate risk. Knowing where there might be soft or blind spots in an organization will equip you and your team with an understanding of what areas you might need to pay special attention to or maybe even ignore entirely.

Opportunities don't necessarily have to be housed in the realm of digital marketing. You want to know what opportunities are available for the business in general. What new product lines might they be equipped to expand into? What geographic regions may show promise? What strategic partnerships are available?

Understanding the immediate opportunities will equip you to build initiatives online that may help drive business value offline. Adding to that, just by asking the question you might end up with valuable insight into where your potential quick wins are.

Threats can be difficult to identify. In an interesting turn of irony, oftentimes a threat is only a threat until it has been identified. The threat stems from the fact that we simply don't see a change coming. I like to think of this section more as "perceived threats," although I typically don't canvas it as that when I'm onboarding Clients.

You can use the threats section to find out what your Client is afraid of. What market conditions or industry changes could have an impact on their business and, by proxy, the digital marketing campaigns. You can also use the stated threats to identify new opportunities.

Product/Market Fit

The product/market fit is meant to articulate the value a business provides by defining the separation in the state of their end user before and after purchase. The degree of separation coupled with the importance of the state that has been changed will define the total value.

The product/market fit that you see in our living plan is a chart that I took from Digital Marketer's Customer Value Optimization (CVO) process. I would strongly recommend investing some time and reading the entire CVO article.

Statement of Value

The statement of value is so simple that it may, at first glance, appear simplistic. The formula that I use (also taken from my training with Digital Marketer) is as follows:

[Product/Service] enables [Avatar] to experience [Result].

What's interesting to me about the statement of value is how few of my Clients have been able to fill in those blanks quickly. Don't let the simplicity fool you. Having a defined statement of value is extremely important and will ensure that everyone involved with the digital marketing campaign is on the same page in terms of exactly what is being provided, to whom and for what purpose.

Explanation of Product/Service

Stating the obvious, you need to know exactly what your Client offers in order to properly market on their behalf. For Clients with products and services that aren't quite as easily grasped, this section will allow you to offer an "at a glance" breakdown of the offering. This is especially helpful when you bring new resources on and need to catch them up quickly.

Competitive Analysis

Identify the key competitors and refer to the list at least once a month during reporting. How well is your campaign performing compared to what you can see the competitor list doing? You'll also want to keep an eye on key competitors to see what they're doing from a marketing perspective. Some of your best ideas can come from competitors. I know this because my competitors copy me all the time.

Remember, a competitor doesn't have to be another business with the same core offer as our own. A competitor is any alternative to your product or service. For example, an alternative to Southwest Airlines might be Greyhound. An alternative to a plastic surgeon could be a gym or nutritionist. An alternative to a digital marketing company might be an outside sales or appointment setting agency.

Alternatives are as important to track as competitors and can be equally as valuable in terms of offering ideas for strategic marketing initiatives. In fact, competing against an alternative in many cases is much easier than competing against a direct competitor. This is especially true if you're in a heavily commoditized industry.

Marketing a gym or personal trainer can be difficult if you attempt to build your value proposition against other gyms or personal trainers. It's not always easy to differentiate yourself enough to compete on any other level outside of price and location. However, if the same personal trainer started targeting potential plastic surgery patients, the entire narrative changes. The comparison between the two becomes so stark that it really helps make the marketing impactful.

Marketing against an alternative instead of a competitive market also helps you market in a silo. Since they're not comparing your costs to an analogous service, there isn't the same challenge of trying to build an "apples to apples" business case. This means you can maintain higher margins and still show huge upside value.

Industry Analysis

To say that every industry is different is a massive understatement. Understanding the nuances of an industry can take more time than may be efficient or effective. However, it's important that you at least have an overarching understanding of how the industry functions, thinks, buys and sells. Each industry has its own culture and you will be ill-equipped to market within that industry if you don't take steps to understand that culture.

One exceptionally important component of understanding an industry is understanding its jargon. Because digital marketing is content based, in a lot of ways one fights a battle of semantics. This is a great opportunity to rely on your subject matter expert. Make sure to ask what industry terms you would be expected to know.

Another critical facet of your industry analysis will be the identification of content hubs. These are trade publications, social networking groups, forums, websites and any other sources of information meant specifically for the industry in question. Identifying these content conduits will help create an immediate list of networks to approach for high value link building, guest posting, authority marketing and direct networking.

Avatar(s)

Where context is one of the most important considerations in digital marketing, the "who" is one of the most important considerations when understanding the context of any marketing initiative. This is an easy place to get a little lazy. We've all been guilty of glazing over the target demographic discussion because, in most cases, it just seems so painfully obvious.

If you have a Client that sells ophthalmic equipment, it would be very easy to simply state that its target demographic is ophthalmologists and then move on. The real question we all need to get better at asking is, who are the ophthalmologists?

We have already discussed the importance of developing an Avatar. Make sure that the work you do in Avatar development is something that makes its way into your living plan.

The Avatar definition you see in my living plan is largely taken from Digital Marketer's Customer Avatar Worksheet.

Regular Management

Rocks

Rocks aren't tasks as much as they are projects. A rock is the definition of a large overarching project that needs to be completed against a specific timeline. I stole the term "rock" from "Traction" by Gino Wickman (a worthy read). A rock can be something like building a website, developing a funnel, creating a paid ad campaign, and other such tasks. The rocks are used ultimately to define the day to day tasks that make up your digital marketing campaign.

While you don't define the minutiae (the day to day tasks) in your living plan, it's important to have your rocks clearly defined so you know what your scope of work is. The rocks are what make up the definition of what you are being paid to do. An excellent way to ensure you're working within the scope of the agreed upon project is to make sure that every task you and your staff perform relates directly back to one of the rocks. If you find yourself doing things that don't relate to a rock, you are off course and need to find a way to correct.

Rocks dictate what you put into your project management tools, how you delegate work, what work you choose to perform and when. The rocks that you define are going to be used on an ongoing basis to help you to continue to drive the digital marketing initiative forward. As rocks are accomplished, mark them as complete. As new rocks are required, add them to the campaign. However, always make sure that what you are doing relates back to a rock. If it doesn't then you either need to kill the task or add a rock under which it can live.

We use a few project management tools depending on Client and project needs. Regardless of the type of tool we're using, we make it a habit to ensure that, whenever we build a task list, every single task has the rock that it relates to clearly defined somewhere. In some tools, it's easy to house a task underneath a defined group; in others we simply add the rock as a tag or in the description. The process isn't as important as the practice.

Milestones

Milestones are wins. They're smaller goals that may not yield any value in and of themselves but which act as indicators of future success. Every milestone you define is the line in the sand that you're drawing on the way to a defined goal. Milestones are meant to act as indications that the campaign is working and you're headed in the right direction. Milestones are excellent short-term indicators that a larger goal is being chipped away against.

In some cases, you can use milestones as a benchmark against which you place future rocks. For instance, we aren't going to begin paid marketing until our email marketing yields 100 new users. The milestone is 100 new users and the dependent rock is paid marketing. Utilizing defined milestones will help you and your team drive towards smaller, more incremental goals when the larger goals may still feel out of reach.

The most common milestone we see is a defined cost per acquisition for paid marketing. The Client won't (or can't) increase their marketing spend until we're able to consistently generate leads/sales at, or under, a specific threshold. Once this threshold is met, we're placed in a position to expand on the campaign in very big ways. I recommend asking this question of your Client: "What would it take for us to double the size of your campaign?" You'll be shocked at how much money you've been leaving on the table.

Tasks

Brace yourself for cyclical logic and a little hypocrisy.

I don't believe in managing tasks within your living plan. Your living plan is not a project management tool. Tasks should be managed elsewhere and simply refer back to the living plan to maintain continuity.

You will notice that, in the example plan provided, there is a place to track the project tasks each month. This is the task list that we use to bridge the gap between the living plan and the project management tool. We reference the rocks and milestones, compare that to the Client's budget or scope of work, and then use that information to build a monthly or quarterly task list.

The tasks that we define in the living plan are what I call the billable tasks. These are the things that we need to accomplish in order to be in compliance with the scope of work. If the Client ever needs to see reconciliation between what they have paid and what we have provided, I can instantly refer back to it in the living plan.

Once these billable tasks are defined, we then migrate them to the project management tool where they are broken down into more actionable tasks. This creates a small layer of redundant work but I'm of the opinion that the extra work is justified by the long-term visibility it provides in terms of project reconciliation.

Another reason that I love Google Sheets is that it allows us to build out the linear timeline you see in perpetuity. We color code the tasks to catalog which tasks were completed, pushed or failed.

When a month or quarter is no longer actionable you can hide those columns in Google Sheets. This allows you to still have access to the data without having to sift through it each time you reference that tab.

What you will find is that you are actually building a campaign narrative naturally and organically when you use this type of process. You'll be able to open the plan in the future and tell exactly what was accomplished and when, this is of immense value when you begin to productize specific services or replicate a successful model for another initiative or Client.

Reports

Your living plan should include the reporting that you deliver to the Client. Instead of sending massive amounts of random numbers, make sure that your reporting is systemic and clearly defined. The data on which you are reporting relates to defined goals, milestones and rocks and is purposeful in its collection.

You don't need to report on a lot of data; you just need to report on the right data. Your key performance indicators are the most important data points to track. After that, feel free to include anything you think worthy of review and analysis that may relate (directly or indirectly) to the campaign as a whole or one of the key performance indicators as a part.

The reporting intervals that you choose should be based upon the needs of the campaign. Longer term campaigns may only need to be reported against quarterly or even yearly. More likely you'll need to report against your marketing initiatives on a monthly basis (as is true with most of your campaigns) or even weekly as with some of our short-term, speculative campaigns.

Regardless of the intervals, the principles of reporting remain the same. Consistency in reporting is paramount. If you aren't able to maintain continuity, you won't be able to compare data over the long term and your reporting will be worth far less. Don't just try to find successes to report against; find what matters and report the truth.

A LIVING PLAN IS A FUNCTIONAL PLAN

HERE I GO BEATING A DEAD HORSE: NOW THAT YOU HAVE YOUR PLAN IN hand, use it! The things that you have written down aren't static pieces of information, they're living and organic assumptions that will change over time. Who your Avatar is will change. Hopefully it'll simply become more and better defined but (in some cases) it'll need to be re-defined entirely. What your goals are may start to change as you accomplish goals and move forward with your projects. Rocks will change or complete and require replacement.

The point of having a living plan is to use it. Your entire marketing initiative should be based on the living plan; it should constantly refer to the plan as an ongoing resource and management tool. As you're working on a Client's project, you should find yourself constantly sharing and referring to the plan with employees, vendors, partners and the Client. If you don't find that happening, then you haven't fully committed to the plan. It needs to be the central point of query for every major decision. This isn't a project management tool, it's bigger than that. It's the thing to which you refer when you're project managing.

Your living plan is what you refer to when you're looking to make a decision, it's what you update when you discover something new and it's what you redefine when you've made a change. If you let the plan die, then you'll be placed in a position of not knowing where you're going or how you got where you are. Accountability gets lost and direction becomes non-existent.

LIVING PLAN AND YOUR CLIENTS

YOUR LIVING PLAN SHOULDN'T BE A "BEHIND THE SCENES" UTILITY. INSTEAD, you should not only make your Client aware of it, but ensure that they're in a position to constantly reference the plan as well. When you deliver reporting, deliver the reports within the living plan. This doesn't just help to ensure you're maintaining continuity, it also forces the Client to reference the plan in order to get to the reports.

The plan will act as a filter for every single Client request you receive. You'll be able to query the plan during check-in calls, strategic planning sessions and meetings. If and when your Client starts to get distracted or attempts to build out initiatives that aren't a part of the core goal, it'll be much easier to shield yourself from the entrepreneurial ADD by constantly referring to the core tenants of the plan.

If your Client wants to add a new initiative, the easiest (albeit somewhat passive aggressive) way to ensure that it's consistent with the plan is to ask the Client where within the plan they see the new initiative being housed. Not only does this help you maintain and monitor the agreed upon scope of work, it can also serve as an excellent ascension opportunity. Just because an initiative isn't part of the plan doesn't mean it shouldn't be. It simply means it needs to be treated as the new and/or independent facet that it is.

Interestingly, the need to keep Clients on track tends to be much more important when a campaign is successful than when a campaign is underperforming or just getting started. Once you start to experience success, your Clients are going to get excited and enthusiastic. This is an awesome place to be and it's so much fun to start to dream and synergize with everyone involved.

However, these new dreams tend to fly higher and further than the original plan accounted for and you sometimes find yourself being stretched too thin. The new initiatives and "fun stuff" that you've added to the campaign start to occupy the time that had previously been dedicated to what had made you successful in the first place.

One very real risk is during each report submission. I have noticed that this is the phase within which Clients tend to ask the most questions and offer the most challenges. You'll find yourself answering for data points that have no bearing on the service you're providing at the moment. When we do SEO for a Client, they will inevitably detract from the list of key phrases they *are* ranking for by bringing up all the phrases that they don't see on the list.

These types of conversations are dangerous because you're forced into a defensive posture and, in an industry of people pleasers, often take responsibility for something that you only later realize was never a part of the plan in the first place. That's why the living plan is so vital. It's an easy reference point for every challenge. Of course, it will change and, in some cases, change drastically as your campaign evolves. But the ability to change is built into a living plan and the dynamism of a living plan will ensure that any changes you make are systematized and rolled out in a way that is manageable and consistent with your processes.

Again, there's absolutely no reason not to grow your digital marketing campaign as is appropriate and conducive to the relevant factors (market, timing, budget, etc.). The point of this section is simply to outline the ways in which the living plan will help to document and effectively manage that growth so that you aren't buried by your successes or distracted by your failures. It allows you to manage expectations on an ongoing basis in a way that isn't combative and helps your Client to realize just how systematic your process is.

USE THE LIVING PLAN INTERNALLY

AS DIGITAL MARKETERS, IT'S VERY EASY TO WANT TO COURSE CORRECT. Because we're acclimated to an industry that embraces and requires constant changes, tweaks and modifications, we fall easy prey to the "this isn't working mentality" of chronic changers and tend to throw the digital baby out with the bathwater when we make a change. When a campaign isn't working or you aren't seeing the results you were expecting, it's easy to want to completely revise and head in another direction. Oftentimes we find ourselves defaulting to where we're most comfortable and trying to compensate for what we might deem as a misjudgment by heading for the quick and easy win. This is a mistake.

If the correction is necessary and consistent with the plan, that's an entirely different story. But don't allow your correction to completely overwrite or even discard the plan. Use your living plan as a constant reference point and reminder as to why you and your staff made the assumptions you made and, along with them, the decisions that you made. Allow them to be an ongoing reminder of your goals, milestones and key performance indicators. Return to them with each proposed change or modification and make sure you're keeping yourselves as honest as you're keeping the Client.

THE LIVING PLAN AS A NARRATIVE

WE'VE ALREADY DISCUSSED THE IMPORTANCE OF NARRATIVE IN RELATION to the human psyche. One of the primary benefits of the living plan is its ability to build a visual narrative of your successes in a way that is easily and quickly seen by the Client. The plan should be structured in such a way that makes historical comparisons and future prognostications visible and measured against existing data points.

You will also be collecting an easy-to-reference list of everything you've done over the course of the marketing plan. As you probably already know, Clients don't realize the immense amount of work that goes into the vast majority of what we do. Building a catalog of rocks, milestones and accomplished goals that is constantly being referenced and reviewed will help to articulate this point repeatedly without you ever having to draw attention to it.

Lastly, when the campaign is deemed a success and you are in effect "done" (or as done as you can ever be in digital marketing), your living plan is now an immediately available case study that can be used internally for education and review as well as provide the building blocks for a public case study (appropriate information redacted, of course).

The living plan will also serve as an excellent reference piece for future Clients and initiatives that somehow relate to the same or similar goals and approaches. Because you documented your assumptions and mistakes, you'll be saving yourself the headache of having to relearn the same mistakes.

ZERO SUM GAME

ONE OF THE BIGGEST ISSUES FACING DIGITAL MARKETERS IS THE LACK OF definition for the term "digital marketer." While you more than likely have a small handful of defined verticals, it's equally as likely that your Clients don't necessarily understand where that definition begins and ends. You may have absolutely nothing to do with the construction or maintenance of the Client's website and you've probably been called (more than once) by various Clients who have website problems and have the expectation that you're their new "everything that happens on the internet" person.

The living plan is an exceptional tool in helping to mitigate this risk. Unlike a scope of work, which could be weeks, months or even years old, the living plan functions as an ongoing documentation of the informal agreement between you and the Client. I say informal because it doesn't need to be notarized and DocuSigned every single time you add something or make a modification. It just needs to be understood by both camps what constitutes an addition or a change.

What's interesting is that you're at more of a disadvantage in this context the more services you offer. If you offer in-house web development services and a Client's site goes down (gets hacked, needs updates, etc.), you'll have far less in the way of plausible deniability than a firm that doesn't even offer that proficiency. The assumption by many Clients is "I'm paying you to handle all of this stuff."

Again, the living plan helps to mitigate this risk to a far greater extent than a scope of work because the living plan has been able to document the agreed upon evolution of your work with the project. That doesn't mean you shouldn't help your Client in emergencies. It simply means you're positioned to provide that help as a value add instead of a service the Client chooses to assume was included the entire time.

Tracking the evolution of the project is important because the chances are it will have to change or even be altered drastically as time goes on. This is just the nature of digital marketing. Where development projects can subsist on a static scope of work, digital marketing will need to allow for changes as part of the plan or find its practitioner meeting with obsolescence as often as not. Because there's often a variable scope of work (or no scope of work at all) it becomes very easy for your Clients to view you as a global solutions provider.

This is perfectly fine incidentally. If you've earned this position in their minds, then you are doing your job. Now you just need to ensure you are appropriately encapsulating your services against the fee you're charging to ensure there's no question as to what's included in the ongoing project and what would be considered additional work. This is less troublesome obviously if you're simply billing by the hour. With that said, I believe hourly billing within the agency model is often a mistake. You limit your ability to profit and scale with a very distinct and stated ceiling. You also limit your Clients and their campaigns by not allowing for the variable of required attention to be an element in the structure of your business model.

With that said, you are allowed to play a zero-sum game. Put simply, if someone is paying you to do three things and then asks you to do a fourth, that's cause for a revision in the agreement. The living plan is going to be your greatest ally in this conversation. Remember, digital marketing doesn't need to be all encompassing. You don't have to assume responsibility for the Client's entire online strategy. If you decide to, you'll probably find yourself in a stronger position in terms of retention and abilities to perform, but that just may not fit with your model or proficiencies.

TOOLS AND RESOURCES FOR BUILDING A LIVING PLAN

THERE'S NO RIGHT WAY TO BUILD A LIVING PLAN. IT'S GOING TO BE HIGHLY dependent on your internal processes and the utilities that you use. I will say that your living plan is not simply your project management tool. While your living plan can live inside your project management tool, you need to make sure it is separated from the minutia and day to day drudgery of normal projects. This will probably mean creating an entirely separate pod, project, workbook, whatever-they-call-it, for each Client's living plan.

Project management tools allow for too much flexibility and tend to get messy. That's perfectly fine, the job of the tool is to manage your mess. This just means you need to protect your living plan from the natural inclinations that are otherwise encouraged in project management tools. I actually prefer to build our living plans outside of project management tools. It causes a small degree of redundancy but I believe strongly that the benefits outweigh the costs. You may disagree, that's fine. It's your business and your tool.

- Here are my personal criteria for a living plan:
- Cloud based—accessible anywhere
- Global visibility—everyone involved can access it

- Change management—track what changes were made, when and by whom
- Gated for security—it should only be accessible to authorized users
- Easily referenced and linkable—make it easy to find and share

You already know my personal choice, and the tool that suits all of these needs to various degrees, is Google Sheets. Using a Google sheet allows you to house an enormous amount of information and to do so in a way that is easily accessible and referenceable. The tabs allow you to break up the living plan into multiple facets or components (depending upon your campaign) and the functionality available within sheets is an excellent supplement for tracking, filtering, formulas and data visualization.

Google sheets allow you to control who has access, track revision history and subscribe to notifications. It also has a unique URL for every sheet so it is easy to share and continuously post to emails, message threads and project management utilities. Because Google sheets are cloud based, you won't have to worry about creating desktop backups or not being able to access your living plan. Google sheets also happen to be free and you can create as many of them as you'd like.

The living plan is going to be built according to your own specifications and requirements. Because every agency, campaign and Client is different, there isn't going to be a one size fits all model. The great thing about using something as malleable as Google sheets is that it'll allow you to easily clone old plans while making continuous and ongoing improvements and modifications. Using Google Sheets (or a tool like it) will allow your living plan to stay alive.

Another benefit to using Google Sheets is the integration available with a vast myriad of other tools. You can integrate directly with a countless number of other applications or use something like Zapier to extend that integration reach even further. This enables you to trigger communication, launch automation, inform and sync data and create tasks automatically.

APPLICATION SUGGESTIONS

1. Build Core Templates

Your living plan is going to evolve. As a matter of fact, if it doesn't change over time it means you're not using it properly. Because this evolution is inevitable, don't try to build the perfect plan up front. Instead, get something started and then work over time to build out a functional plan that serves your core purposes. The plan templates we use will vary from Client to Client based on what we have identified as a Client's unique needs.

As you build additional plans for new Clients, I would recommend having a core plan template that you use to establish some type of baseline. As you make additions to a Client plan that you think are worthy of inclusion in other plans in the future, update the core template. This will ensure that the learning you're doing as you work within your plans isn't lost.

You might find that certain inclusions aren't applicable to every type of Client but are still worth tracking for future Clients of a similar type. Feel free to build child templates that are service or vertical specific. We have a much different plan for lead generation focused campaigns than we do for full spectrum integrated marketing campaigns. Attempting to use the exact same plan template, regardless of application, is going to limit your ability to deliver and track value.

2. Make the Plan a Reference Point

Your living plan is going to be most successful if you're able to get everyone that is involved in the project using the plan. To do this, force compliance by making the living plan a constant reference point. Never pull information out of the living plan to share with others; instead simply reference the information and its location in the plan so you force everyone to get used to querying the plan.

This is true for employees and vendors as well as Clients. When you perform your regular reporting, include anything that the Client wishes to see within the living plan. For example, it is not uncommon for us to need to submit lead reports to Clients. We always place these lead reports within the living plan to acclimate the Client to be constantly checking it.

There are a handful of powerful benefits to having your Clients repeatedly reference your living plan. One of the most important is the ability to provide a constant reminder of what was agreed upon in terms of scope of work as well as key performance indicators. Clients have the bad habit of being entrepreneurs (don't we all?) and will chase new thoughts and ideas with reckless abandon. The more often they see the agreed upon plan, the less often you'll be required to bring them back to center.

That isn't to say that the plan won't change, simply that a change in the plan will be acknowledged as a change since the core concepts of the plan aren't foreign or forgotten. A living plan will also allow the Client to see the changes over time which can have the added benefit of dissuading frequent change requests as they will have very clear visibility into the number of change requests they've made.

3. Using the Living Plan to Develop Case Studies

One of the additional benefits of using a living plan is that you're building an amazing foundation for a Client case study. When you have a campaign that has experienced an extraordinary level of success, you're able to go back and draw on the living plan to view the entire narrative from start to finish. This means that the case study is already complete and you simply need to pretty it up and redact any sensitive or proprietary information.

Case studies make the most amazing marketing content. By using a living plan you're tracking the results over time but you're also tracking those results against the initiatives, tasks and changes that were made within the plan. This allows you to build strong correlations within your case study and explain your process to potential prospects. The case study will also be already built into a narrative format simply by following the chronology of the plan.

4. Try to Identify the Tipping Point with Each Successful Plan

As soon as you've achieved a core goal or milestone for a Client, review the living plan and attempt to identify the tipping point in having achieved that goal. Sometimes the tipping point is obvious.

However, sometimes you might identify something that could dramatically impact your overall strategy.

In reviewing our plans for a recent Client, we found the tipping point in his pay-per-click campaign came when we started heavily split testing his ad copy. We then looked back over previous plans for Clients with similar campaigns and found a similar pattern. Split testing had always been an important part of our strategic approach but we typically saved the deep dive until after we had built out the entire campaign funnel. This discovery led to an accelerated rate of split testing among new plans.

PRINCIPLE 5
USE APPROPRIATE TOOLS
EFFECTIVELY

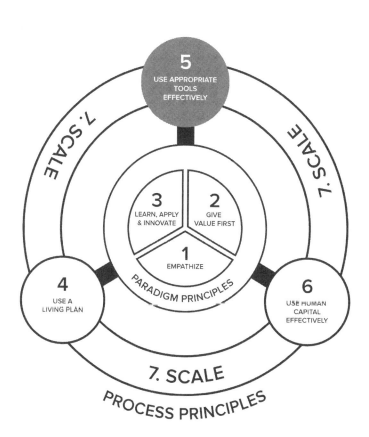

THERE IS AN ALMOST LIMITLESS SET OF TOOLS AND TECHNOLOGIES AVAILABLE to, and in some cases, built specifically for digital marketers: CRMs, marketing automation suites, media creation tools, project management applications, landing page builders, content management systems, integration suites, plugins, add ons, bolt ons and a whole host of other "stuff." The selection, implementation and use of these tools is vitally important to our work as digital marketers which is why it is one of the critical principles of digital marketing.

Using Appropriate Tools Effectively is one of our core principles because doing so will have a direct and substantial impact on every individual marketing campaign you ever run. While I do enjoy the age-old mantra "it is a poor workman who blames his tools," I also know from hard learned lessons that, in so many cases, you're only as good as the tools that you choose to use. The apparent contradiction here is settled when we accept the fact that the workman needs to be responsible for his tool choices. Any blame that then exists will belong to our choice instead of the tool.

Choosing which tools to utilize is the first half of the battle and it is also the easier of the two halves. The real fight materializes when it comes time to utilize those tools. For example, every single website on the planet should have some level of analytics installed. I can't begin to count the number of digital marketers that I have seen routinely ignore their website analytics. They install tracking because they know they are supposed to and then they never look at the data again.

It takes almost no time to set up and monitor goals in analytics. Using that tool would make the campaign owner's life easier on an exponential scale that I'm not mathematically qualified to quantify or calculate. The wealth of data that is immediately available can help drive campaigns toward success and, importantly, to a handful of quick and easy wins on an ongoing basis. You don't even need to dig deep to find it! There's a ton of actionable "stuff" just floating on the surface. So why doesn't everyone use it?

Even when people are using analytics they're not always using them effectively. The dashboard can be a little daunting to navigate and there are quite a few bells and whistles that make it an exceptionally robust tool. However, if you took a two-hour long training course (and there are maybe a million available) you'd be more than equipped to use the primary facets and features of analytics. Instead of just watching data, you would be monitoring it and positioning yourself to make it actionable. It's about tracking the right things in the right ways and it isn't hard once you learn the basic.

This is true for everything, incidentally. We're currently an Infusionsoft Certified Agency and get quite a bit in the way of referrals of Infusionsoft users. Of every single new Infusionsoft account I'm in, 7 out of 10 of them aren't using any of the features that would justify the cost of the tool. I think Infusionsoft is amazing. I'll go as far as to say that it's helped us scale our business beyond what would have been possible without it. I'm a big fan of the tool. With that said, why the hell are these people paying for something they're not going to use?

THE PROCESS FOR NEW TOOL INCORPORATION

THE TOOLS YOU USE ARE GOING TO BE HIGHLY DEPENDENT ON YOUR business model, specific needs, Client base and integration requirements. There is no one-size-fits-all marketing suite for agencies. Because there are so many options available, you'll need to be intentional about how you choose the tools you ultimately end up using. Here's the process I recommend:

Identify Integration Requirements and Specific Dependencies First

Often, you're going to need to purchase a tool that plays nicely with what you already have in place. Before you start looking at potential solutions, make a list of everything that your perfect solution will need to integrate with and/or talk to. This will help you drive the search, inform the conversation if you end up talking to a sales person, and save you from falling in love with a tool only to find out it won't plug and play with your current setup.

When you've defined your integration requirements, it is helpful to use that as the launch pad for your initial search. Quite a few

157

software solutions list their available integrations publicly. This is a great place to start if you have one or two core applications with which your new tool will need to integrate. For instance, if your website is built using WordPress and you're looking for a new form builder, I'd recommend starting your search by reaching out to the WordPress community to ask what form builders are the best and easiest to integrate with.

Identify the Applicable Core Feature Set

Be very clear as to what features are important to you. Make a list of your "must haves" and your "nice to haves" and keep them top of mind. The list can be dynamic. When I'm searching for a new solution, I always end up adding to my list after seeing what is available. I can't count the times I came across features that I had no idea existed and were even more impactful than the solution I set out to find. I like to use a spreadsheet (Table 1) to keep track of the solutions I'm comparing and give me an "at-a-glance" comparison of everything I've seen. It usually looks something like this:

	Tool #1	Tool #2	Tool #3
Price	$500 Total	$10 per Month, per User	$50 per Month
Must Have #1	Included	Partial (Missing "X")	Not Included
Must Have #2	Included	Add-on ($10 per Month, per User)	Included (Light)
Must Have #3	Partial (Missing "Y")	Add-on ($5 per Month, per User)	Add-on ($10 per Month, per User)
Nice to Have #1	Included	Not Included	Not Included
Nice to Have #2	Not Included	Included	Partial (Missing "Z")
Intergration	Complete	Partial (Missing "A")	Complete

Table 1. Table of Core Features

Reconcile your list against your model and make sure you're not shopping for a tool that is inconsistent with your core offering. This sounds like an obvious statement but I have gotten myself into trouble in the past when I start allowing myself to be swayed by features that are of secondary importance to my search.

Demo and Poke Holes

If a guided demo is available, take it. I know it's annoying to talk to sales people and you place yourself in a position to be harassed until you make a decision. However, it usually accelerates the process to walk through the application with someone who knows it. You can get a sense of the company culture and potential levels of support you might expect if you do make a purchase. You can also ask for examples of your specific use case and potentially see a deployment that may be close to yours.

Test Each Applicable Feature Set

Most small digital marketing tools offer a free trial of some kind. Test the application before buying it whenever possible and make sure to thoroughly test each of your required feature sets including (and especially) integrations. Just because an application says it integrates with your CRM doesn't mean it is going to integrate the way you need it to.

We bought a form builder that integrated very well with the CRM our Client was using at the time. However, we didn't test it thoroughly enough before purchasing and found out after the fact that it couldn't pass hidden fields into the CRM. We provided Pay-Per-Click services for this Client so hidden fields were an absolute must to track the campaign. We tested the tool on a cursory level instead of putting a test directly into our specific use case.

Purchase

You would be surprised to find that a lot of seemingly "set rate" tools are negotiable. Before I buy anything I always spend some time researching what other folks say they paid. I'll also Google the name of the tool alongside the words "promo code" or "special." If you want to get super cheap (and I usually do) cancel the tool after the free trial, even if you plan on making the purchase. You'll typically see the last-ditch effort of retention in the way of a price drop.

Training and Accreditation

More and more, tools are offering in-depth training and even accreditation. If you don't have the time to take the training, that should be an indication that this may not be the right time to incorporate a new tool into your system. You can and should delegate this task to the person within your organization who will be most closely associated with the tool. This can be followed up with an overview/pass down for the benefit of the rest of your staff. Regardless of how you decide to approach it, spend the time it takes to learn how to utilize the application to its fullest extent. Anything less is just wasting money and asking for trouble.

Roll Out Plan and SOP

I don't recommend making sweeping changes to campaigns. Trying to roll out a tool to every single Client and campaign is going to force you to solve every single contextual and Client-specific issue you will ultimately face all at once. Instead, I'd recommend choosing a single campaign (preferably one of your own or an extremely low risk Client) and using that roll out to build a standard operating procedure.

As you incorporate the new tool, document the requirements, integrations and necessary steps to fully building the tool into your campaign. In addition to the roll out, spend a month (or as long as is necessary) updating your processes for campaign management to include your new tool. This SOP will continue to evolve as you begin to use the tool extensively. Additionally, you'll put yourself in a position to mitigate risk if you encounter issues with the tool or how it relates to existing processes.

Regular Review (Quarterly, Yearly)

You and your executive staff should make it a habit to review your global menu of tools on a regular basis. If you're using a lot of them, this review might be conducted more often than if you're only using a handful. Look at what you're using to accomplish specific processes and determine if there's anything new that could be utilized that is potentially more effective or efficient.

You need to be appropriately committed to a tool enough to reap its full benefit. However, you also need to be nimble enough to know when a new tool set is worth the time, effort and energy to make the switch. There's no hard and fast rule here. In fact it is an art in and of itself. This is part of the reason you're the expert but it does mean that you are placed in the unfortunate position of having to make these tough decisions.

You won't always choose correctly but you can't allow that to stagnate your business. Once you have done the homework and feel confident you at least understand the variables, then make a decision and commit to it. Oftentimes indecision is the worst decision.

DIAGNOSE BEFORE YOU PRESCRIBE

To a man with a hammer, everything looks like a nail.

- Mark Twain

As YOU BUILD YOUR AMAZING ARSENAL OF DIGITAL MARKETING AWESOME-ness, you may find yourself excited to use everything in your catalog of firepower to demonstrate that you are a force to be reckoned with. This can get even more tempting as you build processes and standard operating procedures around specific tool sets. You have solved a problem by creating a great solution and now it's time to go share that solution with everyone, even those who don't have the problem to begin with. Always ensure that the initiatives you under-take refer directly to at least one of the core goals of the campaign.

Do not let anything be taken for granted when you're building a new campaign. This is easier said than done because it requires a new and fresh perspective with every campaign you launch. Com-mit to being that perspective and you'll benefit every single time. There are no two Clients, campaigns, markets, verticals, prospects or networks that are exactly alike. As such, there should be no two so-lutions that are exactly alike.

Review your toolset against the needs of every new Client and campaign to ensure that you're not building things that are unneces-sary or, far worse, ignoring problems for which you simply don't have a solution. This is why the onboarding process in the living plan is built out the way it is. Before we ever begin talking about tool sets and roll outs, we need to make sure we've identified goals, KPIs and milestones. This is the first step to ensuring that the solution you create is an answer to the Client's specific problem instead of simply the easiest problem you know to solve or happen to have a toy for.

COMMITTING TO A SINGLE SOLUTION

THERE'S ABSOLUTELY NOTHING WRONG WITH BUILDING YOUR BUSINESS ON a platform. I have seen some amazing digital marketing agencies running on application specific consultation. In fact, it's often an easy entry point with potential new Clients. Coming in as a consultant on a specific tool allows you to see the entire scope of the situation without the same veils or layers that Clients tend to put in front of vendors during the RFP process.

For example, I have a close friend and friendly competitor who earns the vast majority of his agency's business starting with Salesforce consultation. The work is exceptionally easy for him to get because he's willing to take the small jobs that don't fit into the hourly minimums of the more traditional consultants who only do Salesforce work. Instead, he uses it as an entry point to introduce himself and his firm to a new Client. Inevitably, every new job leads to a handful of recommendations. As you can imagine, these recommendations often include services that his agency conveniently happens to offer.

Salesforce is just an example. Solution specific businesses can be built on top of literally any tool. The tool's user base and adoption rate will (of course) dictate the viability and scalability of doing so. I spoke with an agency owner recently whose entire lead generation system is based on Facebook pixel installation. While Facebook's new pixel is an improvement on its legacy solution, it has still been known to cause some confusion. His entire entry level business model is constructed around helping people pixel users effectively and then build remarketing campaigns around those pixeled users.

Of course, his business becomes more robust once the remarketing campaign is built. Remarketing campaigns tend to perform far better when the prospect is driven to a landing page than to the home page. Multiple landing pages are necessary if the remarketing campaign is testing multiple messages and oftentimes a lead magnet should be developed. If there's a downloadable offer, you should probably also have an email nurture. You see where this is going—he ends up being the solution to all of these new needs. It's an excellent way to earn new business.

By committing to a specific platform, you will also place yourself in a position of power with that specific tool. You're essentially placing yourself as a power user of that tool. You'll have a broad range of multi-faceted experiences across a variety of campaigns, all with a single tool. This will make your importance to the company that owns the tool far greater than that of a single point of use user. You'll potentially be invited to host user groups, asked to sit in on masterminds and be given the first look at new functionality. In some cases, you'll be allowed to test functionality prior to its roll out and—this is where it gets exciting—even inform and drive new features.

Committing to a single tool set will amplify not only your power but also your voice within that specific vertical. You can do it with every tool type you use. As you grow, this will enable you to better control the environment you're in by putting you in a position of influence with the tools that you are in so many ways beholden to. You'll experience greater degrees of support and, in many cases, more buying power that you can use to increase profitability or pass along to your Clients for greater cost savings.

In addition to everything mentioned above, committing to a single solution (when possible) will help make you and your team better with that tool. As with anything the more you use it the more proficient you'll become. This standardization helps to streamline processes and acclimate your team to your library of core tools.

With all of that said, there's a flip side to the coin in terms of building a platform specific business.

THE DANGERS IN COMMITMENT

WHEN YOU COMMIT TO A SINGLE SOLUTION YOUR BUSINESS BECOMES dependent upon that specific platform not just in terms of the health and longevity of a tool (Salesforce probably isn't going anywhere, at least not overnight) but also in terms of the decisions the company that owns the tool makes. They can kill types of integration, choose to focus on specific verticals or make application changes, additions or adjustments that impact the way your business functions.

If you choose to be a platform specific agency, realize that you're going to end up being more than a service provider for that platform. You'll also end up being the whipping boy for anything that platform does— you become synonymous in the minds of your Customer with that specific platform. You will own the responsibility of having placed your Customers on the platform and, as you will be viewed as the primary salesperson, you will also assume the role of Customer advocate with the company, tool or platform. This can become a sticky place to be.

In addition, commitment brings the obvious danger of your tool biting the dust completely, becoming antiquated, or getting outgunned by a new or better tool. This is a distinct possibility in an age where one small change or new invention can have profound impacts on entire industries. Google has made one-word policy changes in their terms of service that have destroyed entire industries. Not only is this an obvious danger but it is also one that is difficult to mitigate.

We used to recommend a tool called Shopper Approved to our AdWords Clients. Shopper Approved did an excellent job aggregating positive customer reviews. They were Google compliant and the reviews would show up in the paid ads; this would increase the real estate of the ad as well as add a layer of social proof. Google changed the minimum threshold of reviews required to be compliant and it resulted in the majority of our Clients being sized out of the market so to speak. There was no way to anticipate this change, of course, and we had a lot of Clients who lost the ability to benefit from a tool that they had invested a lot of time cultivating.

Adding to the list of dangers is your inability to offer certain types or levels of services. If you have committed to Infusionsoft as a marketing automation platform, it'll be difficult (maybe impossible) for you to take on a Client who has committed to HubSpot as a toolset.

So, what's the right answer? There are a pile of benefits to committing to a single solution but there are enough drawbacks to make you think twice about doing so. I have an opinion on the topic. I'm not going to say it's the only right way but it has worked very well for us.

MARKET BENEFITS, RECOMMEND TOOLS

MY AGENCY IS INFUSIONSOFT CERTIFIED BUT I TRY VERY HARD TO NEVER market Infusionsoft services specifically. Instead, I speak to the benefits of automation from a high-level perspective. I explain the value proposition that Infusionsoft has without ever bringing the tool to the forefront of the conversation. Once I have earned the opportunity to build a proposal and speak to my prospect's specific needs, I make my recommendation to use the tool(s) I feel is best suited to their needs. If Infusionsoft is a fit, I'll position myself as the provider of that particular facet of the marketing. However, I also introduce the two alternatives that I believe are the strongest contenders considering their use case and then have the Client make the decision.

I have had Clients head in directions other than where I led them, but more often they take my recommendation. However, there are instances where it completely makes sense from their perspective to choose another tool. It might be a pricing decision or a matter of integrating with their existing setup. No matter the reason, the benefit I'm left with is plausible deniability because the final decision was theirs.

You will need to price out the service level difference if the Client chooses to use a tool you don't support. If a Client chooses a tool you can't support in-house, it will be necessary to bring in a freelance resource or give the Client the responsibility of handling the management of the tool on their end. This is typically less than ideal but in no way should it be a deal breaker. If you make it a big deal, your new Client will see it as an issue. If your process and paradigms are well built you should have no problems delegating your needs to an effective outside resource.

If a Client chooses an alternative tool, that shouldn't necessarily be an issue. However, if your Client chooses an inadequate tool then I would recommend walking away completely. Using something you're unfamiliar with isn't a perfect situation but it is a problem that can be surmounted. But using something you don't feel fit to the task is asking for failure and can ultimately reflect poorly on you.

DATA AND REPORTING TOOLS

ALLOW ME TO TELL YOU SOMETHING YOU ALREADY KNOW: THERE IS AN unbelievable amount of data and reporting in digital marketing. Obviously, there are data specific tools that are available, things that are specifically meant to provide and/or track data on a particular dynamic of your campaign. In addition to these, there are tools that help interpret this data, integrate other data sets, enhance certain types of data and even data tools that track and report on your data tools.

Add to that the fact that the vast majority of your digital marketing tools, even tools that aren't data specific, are going to report on themselves in some form or fashion. Tool performance is always something that should be monitored and understood. The vast majority of available tools make internal reports at least a small facet of the available featuress.

When you start looking at the data that's available, it becomes easy to get overwhelmed. Now, obviously not all this data needs to be reported on. Doing so would serve nothing but to frustrate your Clients and convolute the digital marketing process with unnecessary noise. However, just because you're not reporting on data doesn't mean that it isn't actionable. The key to utilizing your data tools effectively is understanding which actionable data points will have the biggest impact.

DATA COLLECTION

THE VERY FIRST THING TO UNDERSTAND ABOUT DATA COLLECTION AND reporting is that you can't report against what you don't track. This may sound obvious now but there's not a seasoned digital marketer alive who hasn't had to suffer the embarrassment of being in a conference room and being asked what the numbers are on that super-duper important thing that should very obviously have been tracked only to have to respond with a tepid: "I don't know; we weren't tracking that."

In some cases, you can use supportive data to reverse engineer these lost data sets but I would recommend not relying on that ability if you can avoid it. Just assume everything you want to report on now and in the future needs to be directly tracked and managed as its own data set. This means that you need to spend time understanding and detailing the data points you want now and making strong, educated guesses on the data points that you may want in the future. Lastly, you'll also want to collect data that, even though you might not report on it, will be actionable in helping you to build and modify the campaign.

This means there are three essential data sets to be tracked over time:

- Data you will report on now
- Data you may report on in the future
- Data that will yield actionable results

We'll look at each of those in sequence.

Data You Will Report On Now

To determine the data sets you will report on now, the very first thing to look at is the living plan. Make sure to examine the goals, the milestones and the key performance indicators that you and your Client have identified for the campaign. Now, each of these is in itself a data point, of sorts. However, there are also supportive data points that should probably also be tracked in order to measure the "end result" data points. This is obviously heavily dependent upon the specific campaign and will take time to determine.

The best advice I can give you is to reverse engineer your first report. Mock it up as though you were building your first month's report and then use that exercise to determine the foundational data points you require to reach the numbers you need to report on. As you start to determine what data you'll need, it'll give a clear picture of the data you need to be tracking to build an effective report.

What's interesting about this exercise is that you will very often find that the "missing" data need to come from the Client. For instance, if one of the key performance indicators centers on the Client's return on their ad spend, they'll need to be providing you with feedback data on which leads closed, in what capacity and for how much money.

It has been my experience that very few businesses do an adequate job of tracking post-acquisition lead data. This is typically a good opportunity to introduce your Client to the benefits of a CRM and explain that reporting on their stated KPIs will be heavily dependent upon their ability to provide quality lead data.

Data You May Report On in the Future

Making educated guesses as to what data points you may need in the future can be difficult. The best way I have found to approach this is to look at your future campaign goals. In almost every campaign we've ever built, there has been a phase 2 (and sometimes phases 3, 4 & 5) on the horizon once we've proven concept. Look at the Client's future goals and use them to understand the data points that may be necessary to track. If you still don't know then ask!

For example, if you're not performing SEO for a Client but know that you may begin doing so in the future, begin tracking key phrase data now! Being able to provide a historical basis of comparison for legacy rankings will be a huge value add when you begin working on improving organic search traffic. Additionally, you'll have historic data that give you some insight into the seasonal and cyclical traffic and ranking patterns. These data are invaluable since you'll be able to compare the values from an active campaign to an inactive campaign which should do more to highlight the value in the work you're performing.

Data That Will Yield Actionable Results

There will be data sets that aren't of interest to the Client that are still necessary to track because of the actionable results they yield. This is any information that provides you with an understanding as to how your campaign's prospect is (or will be) engaging with your marketing initiatives.

- Tracking the performance of key pieces of content across social channels may help inform what topics are most relevant for future content marketing initiatives.
- Tracking the highest performing key phrases in a PPC campaign may help inform how to approach an effective SEO campaign.
- Tracking user movement and engagement across a website will provide actionable data on how to potentially conversion optimize the site or landing page.
- Tracking typical device usage will provide insight into your user and how best to engage with them.

While these data points are important, many of them delve too deeply into the minutia of digital marketing to be anything that you make it a point to report on. While your Client may not find these data points quite as riveting as you do, the results you're able to yield by taking the necessary actions against the data will definitely prove to be of interest.

REPORTING NEGATIVE DATA

REPORTING ISN'T SIMPLY A BAROMETER OF WHAT HAPPENED; IT'S VERY OFTEN a road map of what needs to happen. In so many cases the reporting will do the heavy lifting for you if you allow it to. This is part of what frustrates me about digital marketing reporting tools, specifically reports that aggregate data across multiple channels. Currently, their value proposition is that they'll find the positive elements of the campaign across all your integrated channels and generate a report on those elements. This way your Client only sees "the good" with every new report.

First, this is plainly unethical. Cherry picking successful data points isn't producing success—it's just creatively masking failure. This is why the living plan chooses the key performance indicators that are necessary to measure campaign health and measures against the same data points every reporting cycle. By consistently reporting against the same data points and making sure that those data points are the strongest available indicators of campaign health, you are presenting a fair and honest view of the digital marketing campaign.

Second, by not reporting against campaign failures and by masking or ignoring negative data, you're depriving yourself of the amazing opportunity of being told almost exactly what to do next. Digital marketers that feel compelled to hide the negative are looking at their role in an incorrect light. As I have stated earlier, people are paying you to make their mistakes for them. Our job is to unmask the negative. Every negative data point you unmask is one step closer to a well-oiled digital marketing machine.

Obviously, this isn't a ubiquitous truth. If you're driving a paid advertising initiative and all the metrics are horrible, you haven't unmasked anything quite as much as you have simply built a horrible paid advertising campaign. Part of embracing the negative data points is also being confident in your ability to fix them.

The key to making other people's mistakes for them is first believing that you are not one of those mistakes. This means that you can't take on work or perform services in which you are not proficient. If you find yourself scared away by negative data, this is an excellent sign that you or your team haven't yet mastered the specific practice in question. If you're a master, the negative data should be viewed as an insight into potential action. Sometimes it's a viability measure against the Client's business or the chosen market.

If you're afraid that the data in question is going to unmask you instead of a deeper underlying issue, that's a sign that you might not be the best resource for that specific approach. Don't hesitate to bring in outside resources and vendors in circumstances such as these. Do so even if it kills your margins. Not only will you be taking a proactive step to salvaging the Client but you will also be placing yourself in a position to learn from a real-world use case. Find a person or company who is extremely proficient at whatever knowledge gap you may have and allow them to fill it. This doesn't nullify your value, it amplifies it!

CORRELATION ISN'T CAUSATION

IF YOU'VE SPENT ANY TIME AROUND STATISTICIANS, YOU MIGHT HAVE heard this phrase once or twice. If you've spent any time drinking with statisticians, then you've heard it millions of times: correlation isn't causation. The danger in interpreting data is that it is so exceptionally easy to jump to broad sweeping conclusions. All five of my failed landing pages had red backgrounds. Therefore, our target demographic obviously hates red.

These thinly supported conclusions are dangerous because they tend to build on top of each other until you have a house of cards atop which stands your entire digital marketing campaign. The worst part is that, because relying on data patterns like these is habitual, you don't know where the real foundation ends and the house of cards begins. This means that you often end up going back to the drawing board.

Knowing how to identify and utilize actionable data is a skill set that you need to invest in learning. Oftentimes this means knowing how to utilize the tracking mechanism you're using better. In many cases this means spending more time with the problem to ensure you've looked at it from all appropriate angles. Here's a great example:

We were working on top of the funnel marketing campaign for a managed services support company. One of their key content pages had an extremely low engagement rate. The page performance for the entire rest of the site was adequate until we reviewed this key page and found that users would arrive on this page and then almost immediately depart. This was extremely frustrating because it was an essential piece of the marketing narrative and was an important landing page for the campaign. We kept making attempts at conversion optimizing the page to no avail.

We ended up installing call tracking numbers onto the site as part of a separate initiative. What we found out was the page that we had assumed was our lowest engaging page was accounting for an extremely high number of call conversions. Because the campaign was meant to be top of the funnel, we didn't anticipate direct conversion happening so early. The call to action was compelling enough to prompt a conversion from prospects almost as soon as they reached the page instead of following the process of the built-out funnel.

What appeared to be negative data was actually positive. We simply didn't have all the necessary data points to properly track it. Odds are, you're going to make mistakes like this one. As with anything, awareness of the possibility is 50% of risk mitigation. Finding value in data is a fantastic paradigm but be careful of placing too much trust in it or allowing yourself to make great leaps without enough data to support your assumptions.

INVEST IN FAILURE

THERE'S A RIGHT WAY TO FAIL. THE FAMOUS QUOTE FROM EDISON STANDS well here: "I have not failed. I've just found 10,000 ways that won't work." If your reaction to failure is to recede or simply default back to the way it was prior to whatever change caused the failure, then your failure was a complete waste. However, if you find a way to use your failure to propel you forward, to inform your next move, then your failure was worth it.

I won't go as far as to say that your failure was a success. There is certainly no need to lie to ourselves. But you can turn failure into an investment in your future success and, in so doing, make it a success over time. Investing in failure is the best way to hone your skills as a digital marketer. This practice transcends proper campaign procedures and elevates itself onto the plane that positions you for excellence. You're not seeking failure out, you're simply embracing it as an inevitability and making sure to always capitalize on the learning opportunity it presents.

When you stop avoiding failures and begin using them to advance your abilities, you'll find yourself next to unstoppable. If it can be done, you'll find a way. If it can't be done, you'll determine such quickly and efficiently. This is the hardest lesson to learn sometimes. Some campaigns fail completely. Sometimes there's not a way to make it work. The margins are too thin or the market too small. When you learn to invest in failure, you become confident in the lessons it teaches and more equipped to see whether or not another avenue is available at all.

PIXELING

Pixel tracking (pixeling) is a form of data collection. When you pixel a prospect you're collecting data on that prospect for future use. You can quantify the chances that they engage with your brand again through remarketing but you can also greatly improve your ability to engage them with relevant messaging. The pages that they've visited, actions they've taken and media they've engaged with, are all things that you can potentially track using tracking pixels.

As with a lot of data sets, you can't retroactively pixel. You need to install your pixel codes and begin using them as soon as possible in order to benefit from the data you collect. In a realm where empathy reigns, pixeling your prospects will enable you to have a conversation that aligns with their needs and interests instead of blatantly retargeting them with generic messaging.

Pixeling is generally network specific so make sure you begin pixeling users for every available network you may deem worthy of future use. You may begin driving traffic to an online property using Google AdWords only to find that your Facebook pixel audience begins to grow into a viable source for remarketing. The ability to pixel a prospect can be as valuable as earning a new subscriber in the right context. In fact, Ryan Deiss has said that one of the key performance indicators he anticipates companies focusing on in the future will be their cost per pixeled user.

YOU ARE INVESTING IN THE COMPANY AS MUCH AS THE TOOL

YEARS AGO MY AGENCY STARTED UTILIZING A MARKETING AUTOMATION tool called Optify for our smaller Clients. It was an absolute game changer for us because Optify allowed us to do so much of what, up to that point, could only be done with larger and more expensive toolsets. We were able to take Clients who couldn't afford a full-fledged marketing automation solution and still provide them with the essentials.

Optify was extremely cost effective, especially for agencies, and was also very easy to use. Optify allowed us to quantify our value in a way that we simply would not have been able to do without the tool. Clients were happy, we were happy, all was well with the world until September of 2013 when Optify shut down without any notice. So abrupt was their destruction that the company was fielding orders and accepting payments from new customers the very same morning it was frantically attempting to manage its closure. The way Optify made its departure speaks to a complete lack of integrity on the part of the managing members of the company (yes, years later and I am still bitter). Literally overnight, Optify was gone.

The loss of Optify sent us into a scramble. Luckily we had redundancies in place that ensured things like our Clients' email lists and media were backed up, but that was the extent of the silver lining. We lost years of historic data and massive amounts of infrastructure (Optify had landing page development and nurture components) that sent a handful of our Clients into a panic. I'll spare you the sleepless nights my small staff and I spent rebuilding, patching and bandaiding countless campaigns.

The mistake that I made with Optify was a hard-learned lesson. When you commit to a tool or product suite, you commit to the company that owns and manages it as well. You have a responsibility to perform due diligence on these companies to the same extent that you would test their software. If you're going to beta test an application on a single campaign, there's probably no reason to ask for financial statements. However, if you're going to do what I did and begin recommending the tool to an entire subset of your Client base, you better have asked some pointed and direct questions about the company's financial health and well-being.

Even the public information that was available on Optify would have been enough to possibly provide pause. They were a small Seattle startup that was operating on venture funding and had yet to report a net positive return. I'm not sure what kind of answers I would have received to questions about the company's health, but the fact that I didn't even think to ask left me in a position of having to own the failure. Here are some of the important questions that I ask now before we ever roll out a new tool:

- How long have you been in business?
- How many customers do you have?
- How many employees do you have?
- What assurances can you offer as to your financial health and well-being?
- Are you profitable as a company? To what extent?
- Do you make any financial information available to customers?
- Are you currently fundraising? Do you have any plans to fundraise in the future?
- What types of contingencies do you have in place?
- What do you believe are the biggest threats to your company? To your industry?

When you start asking these questions regularly, you will be shocked at some of the answers that you get. You will also be surprised at how much information some companies are willing to share. Obviously, you won't get access to their bookkeeping or last year's taxes. Some of these questions are meant to simply position you to hear the type of response you're given, even if the "real" answer isn't something you expect. There's no absolute failsafe to ensure that you don't end up saddled with an Optify, but there are ways to mitigate the risk.

Writing this, I do wonder whether or not asking any of these questions would have stopped me from signing up with Optify in the first place. I'm sure a slick sales guy or silver tongued executive might have said what was necessary to assuage my fears. Even so, having learned this lesson, I can count more than a dozen instances where this line of questioning has led me to a far better and far stronger decision than having gone forward without it. Don't be afraid to challenge a company, especially if you're putting a large selection of your eggs (or your Client's eggs) in their basket.

THE GAME OF SOCIAL INTEGRATION

JOOMLA IS A CONTENT MANAGEMENT SYSTEM (CMS) THAT, AT ONE POINT, was a very real contender for the industry standard website foundation. Joomla was strong, robust, scalable, open source and relatively secure (as far as open source applications go). In fact, Joomla was the best open source CMS available for website development—a subjective statement but one I stand by.

At the same time, WordPress was a blogging platform that started to outgrow its initial use and began expanding into a more full-fledged CMS space. WordPress was unstable, poorly structured, limited and susceptible to hacks. But WordPress had something that Joomla didn't: it was extremely easy to use. People could deploy and customize WordPress without much training and without any formal knowledge on web development.

In the meantime, Joomla still functioned according to certain traditional development paradigms. It required a certain level of understanding to work with, specifically because it did things "the right way" as far as foundational development approaches are concerned. This meant that, while traditional developers and coders favored Joomla for its strength and foundation, hackers and prosumers favored WordPress for its ease of use and quick deployment.

As it turns out, there are way more hackers than there are developers. WordPress won the game of social integration and became the most widely used CMS in history. At the time of this writing, WordPress hosts almost 70% of all open source CMS sites while

Joomla (in second place) hosts only 11% (Opensources.com, 2015). The reason that this is so significant is because of the strength it would ultimately offer the winning tool.

Developers began building more plugins for WordPress, the community around its core foundation development grew and the integrations available for it grew almost exponentially. In a very short span of time, WordPress became the gold standard for website development. The gaps that had existed with the tool were, for the most part, filled, corrected or at least accounted for. Over time Joomla site owners would find themselves at a number of significant disadvantages.

Joomla was without question the better tool from a technical perspective. WordPress won in one category only and that was ease of use. Because social integration is so important, WordPress won the war in what ended up being an almost non-contentious battle. Joomla ultimately didn't even stand a chance. This is an excellent lesson for digital marketers to learn. Social integration trumps most anything else.

The reason that this is so important is that, where there's social integration there will be support. This is true for open source as well as proprietary initiatives. The more people that use a tool the more time and money will become available to build that tool out. As a digital marketer, you need to be comfortable bowing to some of these rules to ensure you're not putting yourself or your Clients at a disadvantage for the sake of some philosophical pyrrhic victory.

This is a mistake that I made. I continued to build my Clients' websites on a Joomla foundation past the point when it became obvious that WordPress was the clear winner. I think I kept assuming the bottom would fall out for WordPress because it was plagued with so many problems. My stubbornness put me at a disadvantage when I would build marketing campaigns because there were so many awesome tool sets that easily integrated with WordPress but either ignored Joomla entirely or required a significant work around.

Needless to say, I ended up crossing over to the dark side and I'm glad I did. I "get it" in terms of how and why WordPress was able to establish such an amazing foothold and so quickly. And I'm grateful for the lesson it taught me. When I am looking for a toolset, especially in a newly developed space, one of the criteria I use to judge the options is current and projected social integration. Which tool currently has the most users and support? Based on available data, which tool do I estimate will have the most users and support in the future?

There's no way to know for sure, but you're better off attempting to set yourself up for success by making an educated assumption rather than ignoring the issue completely. The ability to integrate with other tools is paramount to a tool's survival in the digital marketing space. Integration almost always requires support from the outside community, whether that is other tools, integration utilities or freelance developers.

I realize it's not any fun to let yourself kowtow to the popularity contests but you'll not be doing yourself or your Clients any favors otherwise. Keep in mind that the numbers game we're discussing here is also a great barometer to keep an eye on in terms of when to potentially jump ship from a tool. If you start to see an application's user base go down it could be an excellent signal to begin shopping for alternative solutions. I'm not saying that is the case 100% of the time but it is a "writing on the wall" situation that shouldn't be ignored.

APPLICATION SUGGESTIONS

1. Best practices for SAAS product purchases

- Try to avoid signing a contract where possible. If there's an incentive to pay for larger terms in advance, then make sure you've thoroughly vetted the product first. However, contracts and long-term commitments are going to place you at a disadvantage in an industry that changes at the speed of light.

- Make sure you understand the pricing model and the implications on your ability to scale. For example, if you're paying per user, what constitutes a "user" and what foreseeable user additions do you see in the future? If I'm placed in a position of having to pay for a new user seat simply to rope in my freelance editor on a single project, that wouldn't be financially sound long term.

- Be careful with white label arrangements. I used to seek out the ability to white label tools, mostly because I liked that it made me look bigger. I would present the tools as "my" tool, as is customary with white labeling, and then be shouldered with everything that comes with owning and managing a SAAS product. I was held accountable for any errors, issues and problems that stemmed from the tool and constantly had to play tech support. I will still white label in certain instances, especially when the construct of the tool set is something I'm interested in keeping private. Otherwise, I see little merit in white labeling and would prefer to have the ability to point my finger at the true source of a problem in the event of an issue.

- Make sure you're exceptionally clear on the support that's available for the tool. More companies are doing a good job at being transparent on this point but I have still encountered issues. There are very large and well-funded toolsets that don't offer live technical support. Needless to say, they don't publicize this fact and you typically only find out after you have a problem. This isn't always a deal breaker but it's absolutely something you should be aware of.

- When you're shopping for a new toolset, especially something that is going to become integral to your business, you can't do enough research. However, the research in this space can be heavily convoluted since there's an entire industry built around comparing SAAS products. As you can imagine, these comparison sites are typically not impartial third parties even when they make a strong attempt to appear that way. I prefer to hit page three or four of a Google search (gasp!) because that'll lead me to reviews that aren't directly attempting to be optimized. You'll end up finding private blogs, forums and other discussion boards about the product and will quickly start to see behind the curtain. I would also strongly recommend looking at sites like glassdoor.com. This is a site that allows employees and former employees to rate the organization as an employer. You'll be surprised at how much information they reveal in terms of what goes on behind the scenes.

2. Become a Power User

This might be one of my best kept personal secrets. As much as I would love to hold on tight and never let it go, I offer it to you now in the spirit of transparency.

If you're going to spend the time, effort and money it takes to begin using a new tool, then I would recommend committing to it strongly. Assign someone from your team as the resident subject matter expert and ensure they have the time and resources necessary to really learn the tool inside and out. Engage the tool's support staff, take all relevant training, get all relevant accreditation, and work to prove yourself as a resource for the tool.

What I just said might sound a little counterintuitive; the tool is meant to be a resource for you. Why on earth would you care to become a resource for it? Realize that the toolset provider is dealing with the exact same target demographic as you are. Their customer list is, far more than likely, very close to your customer list. Further, they're not in the "managed services" business, they're in the software business. Organizations like this seek out strategic partners to which they can refer work.

What's interesting to me still, is how easy it continues to be to earn this position of trust with even the largest organizations. The entire SAAS customer base, as a stereotype, treats them like a provider. They ignore the coaching calls, balk at the certification and tend to be a little less than gracious when there's an issue. On the other hand, my team and I will go out of our way to build this relationship. We write positive reviews and offer to act as references for the sales team. We engage heavily with their support and training staff and try to do so in a way that doesn't make their lives miserable.

In addition, we commit to learning the ins and outs of the toolset and illustrating how we can amplify the value of the tool through what we know about digital marketing. As we build a relationship with the support team and they begin to see how competent we are with their tool and in the space in general, we are almost always (I mean this: **almost always**) placed in a position of referral partner. I have earned some of my best Clients from referrals that came to me through some of the smallest and most obscure channels.

3. Become an Advocate

When you commit to using a tool, you place yourself at the mercy of that tool's success. The more growth the tool experiences, the more users it ends up with, the more robust it will ultimately become. I would highly recommend becoming an advocate for the tools that you use and working to ensure that you participate in ensuring the tool sees growth.

This doesn't mean you need to do free marketing or start knocking on the doors of friends and family trying to sell them your new favorite SAAS product. Simply take the time to write a few great reviews in well placed areas online, recommend the tool when given the opportunity and act as a reference, if necessary.

Oftentimes I see digital marketers (and companies in general) trying to hide the toolsets they're using as though making people aware of them would somehow diminish their own value. This is flawed thinking. Realize the synergistic relationship you're involved with in the tools you've chosen and take whatever reasonable measures are available to see those tools successful.

4. Individual Tools Are Great Sources for New Leads

Beyond making besties with the folks behind the scenes of your various tools, make an attempt to publicize your use of the tools in your arsenal. Again, this isn't something you need to spend an inordinate amount of time on. Just make a few quick videos and maybe a blog post or two on the unique and creative approaches you've been able to take with the tool. Especially focus on specific use cases or problems that you think other people might have experienced.

People find this content! Especially if you're doing something unique or solving a problem others might not have figured out yet. These are excellent lead generation techniques that can easily segue to much larger engagements. Again, a customer who is using the tool is more than likely positioned within a demographic you could potentially service.

PRINCIPLE 6
USE HUMAN CAPITAL
EFFECTIVELY

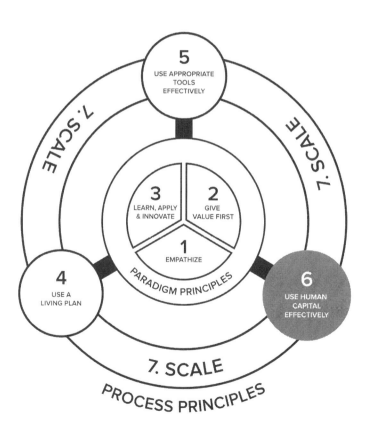

DIGITAL MARKETING MEANS TOO MANY THINGS. THERE ARE TOO MANY tools in the toolbox for any single person to be a one-(wo)man show. Some of you might read this and have no issue accepting that fact. You might even think I'm stating the obvious. I applaud your sense of realism.

To the person who openly defies the statement above and thinks s/he is a one-person digital marketing machine, I beg of you, for the sake of your Clients and yourself, stop being a moron. Yes, you're smart. Guess what? We're all smart. This is an industry run rampant with super nerds. I have no doubt you're capable of anything...truly. However, you're still one person. You still only have 24 hours in a day. You. Can't. Do. Everything.

Even if you could, it's just never going to be as good as if you swallow your pride and start bringing in other proficient resources. This is true for agencies just as much as it is for individuals. I have seen entire agencies run on the single resource model and it's a nightmare. They build their entire marketing platform off the idea that a single employee can handle an entire campaign from end to end. There's no difference between that type of "silo" paradigm and some dude sitting in his Grandma's basement.

Your human capital is the most important resource you will ever have as a digital marketer. That doesn't just mean employees—it means employees, partners, strategic alliances, friendly competitors, vendors, freelancers and service providers. The people that perform the services necessary to your digital marketing campaigns are your most valuable tools. Here's why...

Digital marketing is digital. Blew your mind just then, didn't I? The thing about anything "digital" is that it is immediately com-moditized the moment it is born. Once I build a funnel, that funnel exists forever and can be easily, quickly and cheaply replicated in perpetuity. The same is true for websites, content, media, marketing mechanisms, advertising mechanisms, and the list goes on.

The mechanization of digital marketing begins to dissolve the value in the mechanisms. The tools become so much cheaper than the tasks they accomplish would otherwise allow; this is due to how well they scale. That's why you're able to purchase a piece of software that cost millions of dollars to develop for a few hundred bucks a month.

Because these mechanisms are available to everyone, the only true and definitive differentiator you are ever going to have is your people. Anything you try to add to that list (experience, mission, vision and values, network, background) relates directly back to you or your staff; to a person. Your people are what make your digital marketing campaigns something more than a collection of software strung together according to some arbitrary set of rules.

You need to become a seeker of talent. Consider this one of your personal key performance indicators. This is one of the most important tasks you'll ever have as a digital marketer and should be one of the primary units of measure you use to gauge yourself as whatever combination of digital marketer, entrepreneur and business owner you happen to be.

Talent comes in all shapes and sizes and from various avenues, sometimes from the places you least suspect. If you find yourself working with an amazing freelancer, realize the importance in investing in that relationship and making yourself the type of Client that freelancer will want to work for over the long haul. Pay well, pay on time, be understanding of small errors and supportive with difficult projects. You need to protect, honor and respect your resources just as much as you do your Clients.

I have been using the same video editor for over six years. I found him on a freelance website when an employee of mine called in sick at the last minute and I ended up stuck between a rock and a deadline. The freelancer's name is Dmitry and he ended up being one of the best video editors I have ever worked with. He lives in Eastern Europe (where I would probably expect to pay a fraction of US rates) and charges me at least as much as a US based freelancer would, sometimes more.

But, he's amazing. The quality of his work is exceptional, he's smart, intuitive, proactive and always delivers a better result than I expected out of the order. He doesn't need to be managed, always delivers on time and doesn't nickel and dime me once the price is agreed upon. I haven't employed an in-house video editor since I found Dmitry. Now, I'm not telling you to axe your entire staff in favor of a freelance workforce. Video editing is an ancillary service that we offer in conjunction with our content writing so it made sense for our model.

Sometimes the talent you find will have to be brought in-house. The greatest business development person I have ever known was introduced to me by a Client and friend of mine. He was having dinner at a California Pizza Kitchen and was floored by the quality of customer care he received from his waitress. She made such an impression on him that he thought to bring it up to me in our meeting the next day. He went on for fifteen minutes about her attitude, work ethic and great personality. She was hired before I knew where in the organization we'd use her.

You can't pay for that level of talent. People who have it need to be coveted. The young lady in question would go on to be one of our most successful business development people ever. Incidentally, she now has her own TV show and has outgrown schlepping digital marketing services. This is a risk you'll always run with good people, but it's one that you should embrace. Even if you're simply one of the stops along the way as they find their journey to success, you'll always benefit more from having lost an amazing resource than never having had them.

If you're working with a specific service provider and you notice an outstanding project manager, start requesting that he/she be put on your future projects. When the individual reaches capacity, ask him/her who within their organization they'd recommend. While companies are always going to have a certain culture that can act as a very heavy influence on their staff, you're still bound to find performers within an organization who operate on a higher level than everyone else.

HUB AND SPOKE

WHEN YOU START AGGREGATING TASK-SPECIFIC TALENT YOU'RE PUTTING yourself in a position of having to herd cats. This is in direct contrast to the single-resource method that I so vehemently criticized earlier. Now, instead of a single person spearheading everything, you have multiple people all focusing on their specialty. While this sounds "easy enough" it can be a managerial nightmare if you don't properly account for it.

The most important step to take is to ensure you have proper processes and procedures in place to manage this constant passing of the ball. You'll need to invest in building a project management outline that allows you to follow and administer catalytic tasks and ensure that the campaign doesn't meet any dead ends. Even when this is in place (and even if you're able to automate it to a degree), you'll need to have a project manager in charge of each campaign.

Because the multitude of tasks are typically intertwined and heavily interdependent, you need someone to coordinate everything within a project and to help work the system that you've put into place. You also need someone to act as a Client advocate, internal subject matter expert and champion of the strategic approach that has been chosen. For these reasons, I favor the hub and spoke method of managing digital marketing campaigns.

I realize there's quite a bit of push back to this type of management in any industry. The hub and spoke approach, while effective, limits the quantity of Clients and projects that can be handled when compared to other more "efficient" types of project management. The issue I will take with other paradigms is that without a leader and strong driver, digital marketing campaigns will begin to waver and disintegrate. As we discussed earlier, your primary differentiator is your people; with that in mind it makes sense that your Clients would need a dedicated person to own the success of the campaign.

You need to have someone who intimately understands the Client, their business, their pain points and value propositions, someone who was involved in (or, preferably, even created) the initial strategy and can continue to drive future campaign initiatives based on that chosen approach. This person will be responsible for reporting to the Client and will build a relationship with the Client as he/she starts to understand what is truly important to them beyond what is written on the page.

Having a single point of contact will also allow you to protect your Client from your multitude of resources. While having specialists will ensure you have a more effective campaign, it will also create quite a bit of noise and traffic. This is all stuff from which your Client should be shielded and the single point of contact is the perfect person to do that. This project manager will orchestrate all tasks and communication in a way that allows Client-side involvement to be streamlined.

Additionally, you'll have someone who is able to properly manage the assigned resources. Regardless of whether or not they're in-house, specialists tend to have very strong opinions on things. They're the best in their field and, therefore, want to do it their way, usually rightly so. This needs to be tempered against the overall campaign strategy and the needs of the Client. Just because something is best practice or the right way to do it within a vacuum, doesn't mean that it necessarily works for a particular campaign or a particular Client.

ENABLING AUTONOMY WHILE STILL CENTRALIZING STRATEGY

THERE ARE RISKS IN USING A HUB AND SPOKE MODEL. YOU LIMIT YOUR ability to scale in some instances. You also can clog up your most important resources (your strategists) with work that is well below their pay grades. There are many ways to mitigate these risks, each of which should be modified according to your own approach and unique needs.

First and foremost, I recommend getting a virtual assistant (or even two) for every single project manager in your organization. You may even want to do this for your high value technicians. To allow me to make this case, think about how much you pay each of these people on a yearly basis. Your very expensive and extremely high value resource is probably spending 30% of their day (or more) on tasks that could easily be pawned off on a $10 an hour resource. You can amplify the value of your highest performing resources by enabling them to delegate their minutia.

In addition to utilizing VAs, work to build a culture of autonomy. This should be in your corporate culture as much as it is in your systems and standard operating procedures. Just because you're functioning from a hub and spoke strategic approach doesn't mean that you need to follow that model with every single task. The blog is written and approved, the project manager doesn't need to be involved in reviewing it, sending it to the development team to post, forwarding it to the social team to market, etc.

Each of these sequential tasks can and should be built in a way that enables your resources to maintain an efficient amount of autonomy not just in accomplishing their own tasks but also in catalyzing subsequent, interdependent tasks. Your project manager can now inspect the workflow without being the bottleneck for every little thing. When it comes to requesting Client approval (or even interacting with the Client in general) I do believe a small amount of bottle necking can be appropriate but that is up to you to decide. This advice needs to fit well within your model to be of value.

When a content writer needs to obtain Client approval, I think it's fine for a resource to be able to interface directly with the Client. However, in terms of where that content may be hosted (as a guest blog) or what additional items of content can be created through repurposing, the resource should know to refer that conversation to the project manager. This is a small example from the way my agency model is structured and, incidentally, underscores the value of clear processes. You might have entirely different needs that require an alternative approach. Just make sure that you're allowing for as much autonomy as is reasonable and possible in order to amplify the value of your resources.

The autonomy you're providing your project resources should free up some of your project manager's time but not place him or her in a position of not knowing about a strategic decision or modification in approach. As the champions of the strategy and the Client's cause, they need to be informed to tedium in order to adequately perform their core function.

THE IMPORTANCE OF HONEST EXPERTISE

THERE'S A DEATH RATTLE THAT YOU'LL HEAR OFTEN IN THE REALM OF DIGITAL marketing: "we do that." It's something agency owners say without thinking, even if the service in question is something in which they have no proficiency. Because we've all been acclimated to an ever-changing environment, there's nothing scary about having to learn something new or attempt to secure a freelancer to whom the project can be outsourced. More often, we're the catalysts to the too-long list of services. We immediately offer to take over an entire laundry list of tasks and practices without having a specialist in each of the necessary areas.

The jack-of-all-trades digital marketer is a human punchline we all know well. As an individual, you may have been forced into an area where you're attempting to manage every facet of an integrated marketing campaign on your own. As an agency, you could still be making the same mistake; you're simply spreading it across different members of your team. Blogging and social media are both "content creation" so it would make sense to have your bloggers start to just write your social posts... right? How well does that thinking usually turn out?

The point I'm trying to get across isn't that you should outsource everything or bring everything in-house. It has nothing to do with *where* the resource resides at all. The point is just that you need to use the best resource for the job and each job usually requires a specialist. Every digital marketing service is unique and requires someone with the experience and understanding necessary to properly manage and execute on the strategy required for the campaign.

Search engine optimization is a delicate practice that requires someone with an understanding of all the nuances of the undertaking. Pay-per-click advertising is an entire business unto itself that necessitates a professional capable of understanding not only the best practices but also the extremely complex and often multi-layered tools utilized for each channel. Social media marketing, email marketing, copywriting and graphic design all require their own set of skills and also require a resource who can be considered an expert in their field.

That isn't to say one person can't be excellent at two things (or three, or five, or fifty). I'm simply making the point that the person managing each facet of the campaign should be the best resource for the job, not the best resource that you have immediately available. Digital marketing is a chain of proficiencies strung together and, like all chains, will snap at its weakest link. That means that if you don't have (or can't find) an acceptable resource for a specific service offering, you shouldn't offer that service.

If you're an in-house agency and are committed to managing all of your digital marketing campaigns in an environment over which you feel you have total control, that means you need to hire a person (or team of people) who can effectively service each of the digital marketing proficiencies you're using in your campaigns.

If you're not comfortable with the idea of bringing everything in-house you'll need to find vendors, freelancers and agency partners to whom you can outsource these tasks and campaign facets. You aren't looking for a resource that can "do everything" and to which you can simply outsource your campaign. You're looking for the absolute best possible resource for each of the required campaign verticals.

At this point it's important for you to remember exactly what you're being paid for and where your value lies. You are a strategist. Your job isn't to press the button, it's to know that the button needs to be pressed and then find the best damn button presser for the job. You will drive the narrative and direction, monitor the results, gauge success and steer change. Like a general on the battlefield, your job isn't to fight the battle it is to win the war. Not only is there nothing disingenuous about utilizing outside resources but you are also better serving your Client's needs when you do so.

Utilizing professional resources (compared to trying to do everything yourself or with your existing team) will have the added benefit of properly commoditizing your offering so you know what to bill for various services. If you're attempting to roll a service into your existing offering by bolting it on to another service, it's easy to make the mistake of underestimating the size or scope of the new service.

By securing a professional resource for the service you'll quickly determine what the industry standard price point is and be able to adjust accordingly. Obviously, you'll need to build margin into the pricing to ensure profitability. You should also be able to negotiate agency pricing based on the amount of volume you anticipate doing.

It is likely that utilizing professional resources will eat into your profitability. In fact, your margins are probably amazing if you're trying to do everything with a few maverick marketers who know enough about each service to be dangerous. The issue with this approach is that you're limiting your ability to perform and scale.

Performance is always going to be limited because you'll never be able to experience the strategy you're putting into place coupled with high level execution. The returns you're experiencing now could grow by many multiples if you put the management of individual services in the hands of someone who is a dedicated professional to that specific vertical.

Additionally, your ability to scale is tied directly to your resource bandwidth. When you're already utilizing resources that are required to "know everything," you're placing yourself in the position that any specialized resource you may need will be extremely hard to find. As you grow you'll quickly see that these utility marketers are difficult to come by. Instead, work on building resources around specific proficiencies and then handle the strategy and project management in-house.

Your project management and strategy is a role unto itself and, like everything we've discussed, needs to be a focused role with resources in place that are capable of handling that job specifically. This is one of the few roles that I would recommend always building in-house. The strategy and project management is the Client facing role that truly drives the majority of the campaign value. This is definitely worth investing in.

THE CASE FOR OUTSOURCING

THERE ARE AN AMAZING AMOUNT OF RESOURCES AVAILABLE AT YOUR fingertips. You will be hard pressed to find a vertical or specific proficiency anywhere online that doesn't already have a handful of people specializing in it. These resources aren't your competition, they're your labor pool.

The fact that you "know how to do everything," assuming that's the case, is not a negative by any means. It will ensure you're able to manage processes, drive strategy and ask the right questions. What you need to start doing is using your cursory knowledge on these topics to find someone who is an expert.

You don't need to do this for every single campaign initiative. You do need to do this for the large-scale initiatives that will make or break the success of your campaign. In fact, I would caution very strongly against the idea that you can prove concept first and then bring in a specialist if the chosen vertical shows promise. I contend that the proof of concept could hinge directly on whether or not the practitioner is an expert.

One of the best examples I can offer you is in Google AdWords. Anyone can run an AdWords campaign. If you have moderate computer proficiency you can probably open the AdWords dashboard now and Forest Gump your way through learning how to build, launch and monitor a Pay-Per-Click campaign. There's a ton of education online available to help you and some of it is actually really good. There are even automated programs you can purchase to help you streamline your setup and management.

I'll take that a large step forward in saying that anyone can get AdWords Certified. The Certification isn't a joke by any means, it requires some real understanding of the process, dashboard and toolset. However, anyone willing to spend some time learning these things is virtually guaranteed to become AdWords Certified. What you will find is that there's a massive difference between an AdWords consultant who "figures it out" and one who really knows what he's doing.

The AdWords team we use is in the Top 3% of all AdWords Certified Agencies worldwide. They're Google Premier Partners and the work they do is nothing short of extraordinary. We run all our AdWords Clients through them and we are able to boast some of the highest performing campaigns I have ever been privy to.

Here's what's interesting: because we're offering full spectrum digital marketing and our AdWords team is specializing in a single vertical, we're able to amplify their value. That means that our Clients benefit from their skills more than they would have had they gone directly to them. Our full funnel marketing approach, conversion optimization and marketing automation amplify the pay-per-click model by many multiples.

This is true for every service we offer. The Agency that manages the backend of our SEO machine (we do the content creation in-house) is an Inc. 500 Internet Marketing Company and amazingly proficient at organic ranking and optimization. They're able to produce a level of results that exceeds what we could ever do in-house and they do so with a set of systems and procedures that would have taken us years to learn and build.

To pile on top of the point I'm making, SEO and PPC are changing every single day. By using resources that are dedicated to a single proficiency I'm making sure that we're keeping ourselves ahead of the curve and not putting the onus of having to learn every nuance to every digital marketing industry on us. My job is to manage the experts, and ensure they stay on top of their game.

Don't worry about being "cut out" or placing yourself into a position of obsolescence. As long as you bring the core value of spearheading the overall strategy you remain the single most important piece of the strategic puzzle. In fact, most of the "button pusher" providers are not strategists (oftentimes by their own admission). You'll find that they need you as much as you end up needing them. And while you will find that this strategy cuts into your margins, the scalability of the model and the success of your campaigns will more than compensate for that short term loss by enabling greater long-term growth.

What you choose to outsource and what you choose to keep in-house is going to be completely dependent on what you're already good at, what types of Clients you're attracting, what your offering looks like and how you approach your strategy. No matter what you choose to keep and what you choose to delegate, just make sure that the best person *for* the job *has* the job. If you want to keep SEO completely in-house you need to find, hire and train the best SEO team on the planet. For some of us, that's far too daunting a task. For others, it's why they got into the business.

The point is that you need to use experts in the field where appropriate and you need to make sure that you aren't the weak link in your own strategy. I can think of no greater tragedy for a digital marketer than to be the reason his campaigns are failing. The strategy you define is going to rest in the hands of the resources you allocate to it. Realize that attempting to pinch pennies, expedite turnaround times or simply maintain control by utilizing a less-than-ideal resource is going to place your entire campaign in jeopardy. And, as you should already know, if the campaign is in jeopardy, so is the entire Client relationship.

You have a responsibility to your Client to make sure that their campaign is managed by the best possible resources considering their budget. I bring this up because I have seen a lot of agency owners and digital marketers act as if bringing in outside help is somehow disingenuous. Nothing could be further from the truth. You are doing your Clients a disservice if you're attempting to handle everything their campaign calls for out of some misplaced belief that they require a complete in-house solution.

The in-house solution paradigm is antiquated and unrealistic. This is true for large and small agencies alike. You can't be the best at everything, it's truly not possible. Even if it were possible, it wouldn't be profitable. If someone else has already figured out how to do it faster, better and cheaper than you, why on earth wouldn't you just outsource it to that guy? The time, effort, energy and money you would use in reinventing the wheel almost always exceeds the cost of just buying the wheel. If that's not true, then move forward with your wheel R&D with my blessing. Otherwise, learn to delegate the right way and bring in experts wherever they are needed.

INVEST

WE'RE CONSTANTLY TRYING TO TELL CLIENTS (AND PROSPECTS) THAT THEY need to look at marketing as an investment and not an expense. As an expense, it's the first thing that gets cut when a company runs into cash flow issues and tends to be looked at as a vanity play. As an investment, it's understood as the lifeblood of all new business and becomes something that people within the organization look to expand at every opportunity.

You need to assume this same exact mindset. When you're performing digital marketing on behalf of a Client, it can be tempting to try and find the most "cost effective" resources available for every task you choose to delegate. There's nothing wrong with this from a theoretical perspective. If a task is well defined and easy to direct, by all means, get it done on the cheap and work to broaden your margins.

However, these menial tasks aren't the only thing we have the bad habit of sending to bargain basement vendors. When you place something that is truly a cornerstone piece of the campaign in the hands of the cheapest vendor, all you're doing is falling victim to the expense vs. investment mistake. You're viewing the task completion as an expense and attempting to cut costs as much as possible. However, if you start looking at it as an investment (and it is), you'll quickly see that you're not putting enough into it to be able to see any level or degree of return.

One good example of this is content creation. I walk around in a state of constant depression when I start to think about how little respect people have for quality content. The internet is nothing more than a conduit for content dissemination. Digital marketing is content marketing. And yet the very same people that ring these clichéd bells and espouse these ideas publicly, will turn around and start ordering their copy from content farms at $0.02 a word.

If this sounds like you, I have a very respectful request to make:

STOP—DOING—THAT.

If your content sucks, your campaign will suck. Even if the content is technically proficient, gets the point across and has no issues or errors, you're still lacking the unique voice and personality that a truly amazing writer will bring to the table. You can absolutely make a campaign scoot by on mediocre content. However, that very same campaign with truly remarkable content is going to soar!

This is where you need to start looking at your own expenditures as investments. Yes, paying more for content means you'll be taking less money home. However, that investment is going to pay off within the campaign for weeks, months and maybe years to come. This is the very same campaign on which you're staking the future of a Client relationship. Think big and sacrifice a little profit now to cement a long-term relationship and reap the rewards for much, much longer.

If you invest intelligently in your campaigns you will see the returns. Another great example of this (along the same lines) is in landing page development. The landing pages are the bottleneck of traffic and conversion. The success of your entire campaign usually hinges on your landing pages and whether or not they're able to convert. So, if you're jumping on Fiverr and kicking your landing pages at the cheapest resource you can find, I hope you are comfortable with disappointment.

This is true for everything you might delegate: paid ad management, SEO, email marketing, data collection, funnel building, etc. Hire the best resource that the campaign can afford and invest in the long-term success of the campaign. While this might eat into your margins in the short term, it'll virtually guarantee you a Client for life.

I realize that this isn't always possible but, just to give a sense as to how important this is, my agency usually isn't profitable for the first three months of a new campaign. We spend everything we can on ensuring we build the perfect foundation in order to position ourselves for long-term retention and ascension. Needless to say, you can only take this approach with the right types of Clients. If you're onboarding Clients without the ability to scale or who might not be the right fit, you're placing yourself at risk. This is another reason to only take on the type of work that you feel fits perfectly with your business model.

Another fringe benefit of hiring experts is it ensures that you're charging enough in the first place. If you're billing an amount that doesn't allow you to hire an expert to perform the work, that should be a red flag that you're not charging enough for what you're offering, or that you're offering too much. In some cases, we have the bad habit of throwing in an add-on service that sounds "easy enough" only to find out that it requires more management than we realized.

I'm not saying that you need to pay more for the sake of paying more. There's no need to hire the sky rise agencies with the high overhead and inflated egos. Sometimes the best resources are independent contractors that are working from home. Your job is to spend the time and effort to find these people and then hang on to them! There's very little in digital marketing that's as valuable as a solid vendor.

As you build your book of vendors and resources, I recommend protecting yourself on both ends. Your Client engagement letters should include no-hire clauses and your vendor and employment agreements should include non-solicitation clauses. Sadly, this isn't going to protect you from everyone but it'll at least stand as a defensive barrier. Because it would need to be breached by both parties for you to be cut out of a deal, it makes the likelihood of that happening far less likely.

DELEGATE

CHOOSING WHAT TO DELEGATE, WHAT TO OUTSOURCE, WHAT TO KEEP in-house and what to keep on your plate is something that's going to be heavily dependent on your personal setup as well as the particular campaign in question. Before delving into the specialty tasks, let's get some of the easy stuff out of the way. You should always delegate the tedious, routine tasks. If these tasks can't be automated (which we'll discuss more in the 7th and final principle: "Scale") then push them off to a virtual assistant.

Delegation still requires management but, assuming your VA is effective, it'll cost you a fraction of the time to manage as opposed to attempting to do these rote tasks yourself. Make sure to always inspect what you expect and continue to check up on your VAs work, or delegate that to someone else if necessary. While utilizing a VA might seem like a luxury, it's really simply a solid cost savings strategy that enables you to scale with greater ease. It allows your more expensive resources more time to work on the tasks that are specific to their specialty.

Outside of menial tasks, I believe that you should strive to keep strategy and reporting on your plate (or on the plate of the dedicated project manager assigned to the campaign). You can delegate sections or areas of your reporting to various resources. You can use what they provide to create the larger report but the report that is delivered to the Client should be created and reviewed by the same person who is responsible for the strategy. Otherwise, the strategic approach will no longer synchronize with the actual campaign which would be a catastrophe.

APPLICATION SUGGESTIONS

1. Track Your Hours

Sounds like fun, right? This isn't something you need to do "forever." However, for just a few weeks I recommend tracking your hours against the tasks you perform each day. I think what you'll find out is that you spend a surprising amount of time on tasks that aren't associated with your core business. Even worse, most of these tasks are far below your pay grade. You're not saving money by performing these tasks! If your time is billable at the rate of $150 an hour, you lose $135 for every hour you work on a $15 an hour task.

After you have tracked your hours, take inventory of everything you do that could be accomplished by someone else. Prioritize the list with the biggest time eaters at the top. Now it's time to go shopping! Hit the Google machine and your freelance sites of choice (craigslist.com, freelancer.com, upwork.com, outsourcely.com) and start looking for replacement or supplemental resources.

Realize also that something that takes you two hours might take a professional or a company a quarter of that. They have the processes and experience necessary to streamline tasks that don't come as easily to you. One of the best examples I have of this is bookkeeping. I see so many business owners doing their own books and it's painful to watch! Go hire a company like bench.co or Powered Books. For a couple hundred bucks you'll have an entire bookkeeping department on your side.

You may also find that you're performing tasks that could easily be automated or that a technological solution could at least abate or even completely subvert. If you spend a large amount of time scheduling meetings and calls, then invest in something like Calendly or Time Trade. If you have a personal or business need that requires you to have constant updates on specific information, spend some time building out a feedburner.

If you find yourself spending more time than you would like in meetings, look into ways of automating the aspects of the meetings that are always the same. This will let you keep meeting time to a minimum and maximize the value of the time you spend in those meetings. You can build an automated email track that prompts everyone to submit their topics for discussion to a central repository and even review all the submitted topics prior to the start of the meeting.

Tracking your hours enables you to get clear visibility on how you are using your time, The reason I think it's important to track your hours is because I don't believe that most of us have a clear understanding of how we do spend our time. I think you'll be surprised at what you find, especially if you're diligent in collecting the information. Just keep a notebook on your desk and jot down what you did every hour, on the hour.

2. Fiverr

Spend some time getting lost on Fiverr. This site is an absolute gold mine for efficiency hacking! The nice thing about Fiverr is that it's a lot like having a brainstorming session with a whole group of other people on what they think you might want or need to outsource. You'll see what people are able and willing to do and so much of it is stuff you never would have thought about.

The site addresses basic things such as data entry and general VA tasks as well as more advanced services like cleaning up audio files and going through job applications. Chances are you're doing a combination of basic and slightly more advanced tasks that could easily be handed off to a dedicated resource. You might need to test a few out before you find the perfect solution, but the time you spend testing will be worth it!

3. If I Weren't Here...

Spend a day (or week, or month) and with every single email that enters your inbox ask yourself the question: "If I weren't here, who would be handling this?" What you might start finding is that there are tasks you're doing or projects you're poking your nose into, that are better accomplished by someone else on your team! You may also find that you don't yet have that "someone else" but want/need one.

4. Where Are the Fires?

Make a concerted effort to track when and where there are problems, such as problems with campaigns, Clients, vendors, technology and employees. If you start to see common denominators with the problems you're experiencing, it may mean you need to find a resource to which you can delegate that specific task.

When we first started with Facebook marketing (before they changed their pixel tool) we kept having issues with installing the pixel. After a few occurrences of this I roped in an outside resource specifically for installing and testing the Facebook pixel. He was usually able to do in a matter of minutes what had taken us a few hours.

5. Grade Yourself

Spend some time reviewing the services that you provide. Write down each of the services and then assign yourself a letter grade in terms of where you think you rank in your market. Chances are, if you're being honest, you have some letter grades that span the spectrum. You might be an A+ in content creation and funnel building but a C- in website maintenance or SEO. You don't need to grade yourself on every digital marketing service, just the services that you provide.

Once you have your letter grades, put your list in order with the worst grade on top and then go shopping (again)! Try finding competent and reliable resources to which you can start outsourcing those tasks. I would especially recommend that you seek out strategic partnerships with other agencies. I say this because there's usually a fair degree of common denominators in terms of what certain agencies are good at.

Agencies with excellent technical acumen may have some shortfalls when it comes to certain creative endeavors and vice versa. If you can find an agency that excels at what you're bad at, I wouldn't be surprised at all to learn that they need help with the stuff you're good at. This type of synergistic relationship is ideal and helps build reciprocity into the relationship.

PRINCIPLE 7
SCALE

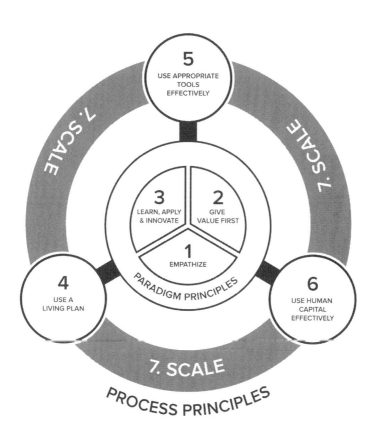

A CAMPAIGN BECOMES TRULY PROFITABLE WHEN IT IS EQUIPPED TO SCALE. Scale is the combination of synergy, integration and automation. These equal components of scale are the key to amplifying the value that you create within your digital marketing campaigns. You have probably noticed that you're already doing a significant amount of redundant work. Beyond redundancies, you're performing tasks and creating content and media that could very easily be utilized across other channels and in conjunction with other efforts.

This proves to be especially true for larger teams or for digital marketing campaigns that involve multiple vendors or resources. The lack of coordination when multiple drivers are involved in a single campaign (or even different but related campaigns) usually means that excellent opportunities for amplifying the value of work across other channels are missed completely.

DATA AND LEARNING LESSONS

ONE OF THE FIRST AND MOST IMPORTANT AREAS WHERE INTEGRATION IS absolutely essential is with the data driven decisions you're making throughout the campaign. If you run a split test against various email subject lines, it stands to reason that the winning subject line might yield results as to which key phrases and buzzwords your Avatar is most interested in. This information could be invaluable to your social media marketing team for social posts as well as your content creation team (assuming they're different folks) for blogging and press releases.

How you choose to share this information is heavily dependent on the data, vertical and method of learning. One great practice I follow is to keep a section reserved in the living plan for things we have learned about our Avatar. Obviously, you don't want to include every test you've ever performed. However, when you do make a discovery that could be applied to other channels and that appears to have significant enough impact, make sure it finds its way to the definition of the Avatar. This evolution of the Avatar will help every-one grow in terms of their understanding of the Client and their Avatar's needs.

Make sure to share notable failures with your team as well. It's important to share this information in the right context of course. But, proper qualifications aside, it's just as important that other team members understand what not to try as it is for them to know what works. The decisions you're making, even failed decisions, are coming from a place of logic and intuition. It makes perfect sense that mistakes would be repeated if their existence isn't commonly shared with the group.

Cross pollinating decisions is a little more difficult if you're not performing the work in-house because you have less control over the processes your vendors and strategic partners may be using. However, it's not impossible and is truly worth the time and effort it will take for you to ensure that this information is shared and utilized among everyone involved in the campaign. Ideally these strategic resources have access to the living plan and are tasked with constantly keeping themselves up to date as well.

One of the most difficult types of campaigns to manage is one where various campaign initiatives are sprinkled across multiple "outside" resources, meaning resources that aren't of your choosing. For example, your team is managing certain aspects of the marketing campaign for the Client, the Client has subsequently chosen to keep performing certain tasks in-house and is also outsourcing other tasks to a third resource to which you have very little access.

In these circumstances, I choose to make the Client responsible for adequately cross pollinating the key decisions across all campaign initiatives. I make it clear how important the practice is but also explain that the structure of the campaign's execution is such that it makes more sense for them to be the driver of the cross-pollination initiative. I'll empower them with our resources and standard operating procedures for doing so and even follow up regularly to see if they're having any issues.

As I'm sure you can imagine, pushing the integration and synergy of ideas is far more difficult when you're not in control of the project as a whole. While it's still important, you will find yourself identifying certain points of diminishing returns when trying to force this initiative through. If you meet with whatever you decide is "enough" resistance, then it might be worth trying to make the case for total ownership in terms of who is running the campaign.

The inability to cross pollinate decisions and learning lessons is an amazing and very specific use case to offer Clients as to why it's better and more effective to have you in the driver's seat completely and allow you to take total control of the digital marketing campaign. Clients aren't always receptive but it allows you to contextualize the issues associated with fractured initiatives and put a face on a very big piece of the problem puzzle.

INTEGRATED MARKETING

INTEGRATING YOUR MARKETING SERVICES IS GOING TO BE AN ESSENTIAL practice if you have any plans of conducting long term, recurring marketing campaigns on behalf of your Clients. Simply attempting to produce "valuable content" on an ongoing basis is going to feel a lot like chasing your tail after a while unless you're able to build logic into your approach and coordinate your team's efforts for maximum efficiency.

Even if you're not building long-term marketing collateral, an integrated marketing campaign will help ensure that all your resources are heading in the same directions. You'll also find integrated marketing efforts will amplify the value of your work and avoid redundancies by yielding logical paths to the creation and development of specific campaign components.

CONTENT REPURPOSING

CONTENT REPURPOSING IS SIMPLY TAKING A PIECE OF CONTENT THAT YOU have already created and having it modified to fit another distribution model or channel. Repurposing content is easily one of the best and most effective ways of amplifying the value of your marketing initiatives. It's extremely easy to do and allows you to profit from the same piece of media or collateral in a variety of ways. The vast majority of the time involved in creating high value content is in the research and preparation. It would be a shame to only yield a single piece of value from all that work.

You're probably already doing some content repurposing. The hope would be that you build it into your systems as a standard practice for great performing content. The very first note of consideration I would offer when working with content is not to repurpose content that you haven't launched yet. If the content isn't going to perform on the channel you initially chose for it, it doesn't make an exceptional amount of sense to attempt to run it on ancillary or vertical channels.

Another note of caution I will offer is to never make the intention of repurposing your content drive the way that the content is made or what types of content you start with. For instance, a blog might be an easier piece of content to create than a video. However, if the situation calls for a video or a video will simply be more effective/appropriate, then create the video.

Always start with what the campaign needs. Don't create content to suit your schedule, your bandwidth, or your available resources. Create the content that you think the campaign calls for at the time. Once that content is complete and goes live, monitor its efficacy to determine whether or not it's a prime candidate to be repurposed into other potential channels.

When you monitor a piece of content's engagement, it's important to realize that the content can fail but still show successful engagement. If an email has an extremely high open rate but low click through rate, it might be safe to assume that the topic was of great interest to the reader but our execution or call to action might not have been properly placed. Maybe the call to action is more complex than is appropriate for a text heavy email and might be better served as an infographic.

The same example holds true for on-site content. When I see pages on a website that have relatively high traffic but also have high bounce rates, my automatic assumption is usually that the promise of the content outweighed the value of the content that we provided. These tend to be excellent opportunities to repurpose content and attempt to amplify the value of what you already have. In this instance, I might add a video or slideshow to supplement the copy.

In addition to using content repurposing to increase engagement on underperforming assets, you should be using content repurposing to amplify the value of your well-performing assets. Assume you have a great social media post that gets awesome engagement; people like, comment on and share it in exactly the manner you were hoping for. This is the perfect opportunity to segue this content into other channels. Some questions you may ask yourself:

- Can the topic be expanded into a blog or article?
- Is this an appropriate infographic, custom image or meme?
- Would this work as a video or slideshow?
- In what other marketing channels can I utilize this content where it might have the same effect?
- Is there a second part or next phase to this content that I should consider?

Find your most trafficked blogs and articles and build a repurposing plan to amplify that content across multiple channels. Here's an example of a potential content repurposing sequence:

- The right, content-rich blog can typically be turned into an awesome infographic.
- Your infographic can be split and sequenced into slides for a great slideshow.
- The slideshow can be easily made into a video with the addition of music and a voice over.

From a single piece of content, you were able to yield three additional high-value assets. All three of these new assets can be utilized across all your social media channels. You can also use them to populate media-specific channels like Pinterest, SlideShare, YouTube and Vimeo. Additionally, media makes for a much more attractive guest posting if you're searching for high value thought leadership opportunities with other websites.

You can build standard schedules for content repurposing depending on your available resources and the way you approach content creation in the first place. Again, make sure this isn't done at the mercy of what the campaign needs in preference to what you're capable of. However, once you have the piece of high performing content you want to repurpose, it makes perfect sense to build a standard operating procedure for doing so.

This will vary based on the campaign's construct and how you create content within your agency. As an example, we had a Client that used to record two to three videos a week on the state of the precious metals market. This was an initiative he started on his own and was already running when he brought us in to help manage his larger marketing efforts. We took the videos with the most engagement and used them to create blogs, guest posts, infographics, lead magnets and in some cases, even press releases and white papers.

Content repurposing is also an excellent opportunity for ascending your Client into a superior service package. For Clients without a robust content plan, I like to do a first round of repurposing for free and then surprise a new Client to show them the capabilities of the repurposed paradigm. It helps to amplify your value as a service provider while, at the same time, quantifying the amount of value the Client gets for their spend. It's a true win/win and, in keeping with our principles, enables you to make a deposit before submitting your "ask" for additional business.

SYNERGIZE 1 + 1 = 3

SYNERGY IS THE CREATION OF VALUE THROUGH COMBINED EFFORTS WHERE the value of a combination of efforts is worth far more than the values of their independent parts. Said less like an idiot, synergy is anytime 1 + 1 is equal to more than 2. Campaign synergy is sometimes a difficult ideal to reach for. This is especially true if you have multiple resources you're attempting to coordinate across various channels. Often I believe that we mistake continuity for synergy. Continuity is exceptionally important and, in many cases, continuity can lead to synergy. However, continuity alone doesn't constitute synergy. I'll give you an example...

Assume you're running a content marketing campaign on a topic. If your email marketing team, your social media managers, your copywriters and your paid ad management team are all pushing the same general message, that's continuity. Again, this is extremely important in and of itself and oftentimes just getting to this point is difficult.

Synergy is achieved when each of those channels is able to utilize its unique power to amplify the work being done on the other channels.

- If there's a campaign narrative or timeline, then each of the channels is speaking to the same phase of the narrative at the same time.
- If there's a logical sequence of content ascension, then the channels are working together in a way that drives customers through that sequence.
- The channels will utilize and capitalize on their own strengths and then call upon their sister channels to supplement or even account for their weaknesses.

If you're running a timed email nurture meant to market a specific offer, continuity would be making sure your social posts are offering the same offer. Synergy would be adding a call to action in your emails for subscribers to follow your social channel if they want more "real time" updates. You could also offer email notifications as a call to action in your social posts for followers that want direct updates that they won't risk missing. Each of the two initiatives helps to amplify the other's reach and efficacy.

Continuity would be running remarketing ads to prospects who have engaged with your brand in some way. Synergy is running remarketing ads that are specific to the products or services they engaged with and modified based on where they are in the funnel. You can build logic into the remarketing ads using conditional dependencies in remarketing (if the prospect has done *this* but not *that*). If the prospect has engaged with your blog but hasn't yet been to your services page, then deliver a lead magnet instead of a trip wire. If a prospect has made a purchase then deliver the next logical value optimization ad, etc.

Synergy is going to be heavily dependent on the needs of the campaign and the approach you're taking with your marketing. If you're running heavy lead generation campaigns to cold traffic, then a synergistic approach would be making sure that the brand presence you're building outside of the paid ad campaign is something that speaks to and supplements a top of the funnel prospect. Because users tend to research the companies they may engage with, you'll want the content they "stumble upon" to be relevant to the ads they've been seeing.

Synergy doesn't always have to relate to the customer or user experience. In many cases, you can achieve a synergistic model by utilizing a piece of content for multiple purposes. In fact, content repurposing can definitely be a form of synergy. Through content repurposing you're building more content with less research and output so the 1 + 1 = 3 model stands very firmly on the practice. However, you can further synergize your content creation by making a single piece of content perform multiple functions or provide multiple tiers of benefit.

For example, if you're engaging in ongoing content marketing, it typically makes great sense to couple it with search engine optimization. SEO is rooted in high value content so when you're performing content marketing, you're already doing a substantial amount of the work required to properly optimize your site. It will require you syncing the two proficiencies in a way that is complimentary but, if it can be done, you'll ultimately benefit from two exceptionally important and high value campaign initiatives at a fraction of the cost of their individual sums.

Synergistic approaches are difficult to define because they usually require a certain amount of creativity and insight into the specific needs of the campaign. There's a great and very simple form of synergy I learned from a Client that we still use for our customers today. He was utilizing his highest performing email broadcasts to string together his email nurture for his engagement series. He was sending the broadcasts independent of the nurture, then utilizing the data yield to build a high performing engagement series.

What synergy means to you, your Customer and your campaign are going to vary greatly case by case. The important thing is making sure you build the concept of synergy into your psyche and that of your team. Always be on the lookout for the ability to combine or amplify efforts for an amplified yield. Synergy doesn't need to be difficult or large scale to be impactful. Some of the greatest exponential yields we've seen from synergistic execution came from the simplest approaches. Utilizing paid traffic data to inform SEO processes is a form of synergistic application that we've used for years and it has saved us and our Clients an amount of time and money I'll never be able to quantify.

Synergy isn't always possible. In fact, automation can be the enemy of synergy in some cases. This isn't necessarily a bad thing; it just means you'll need to make a strong decision as to whether or not the ease and scale produced through automation is worth the potential trade off in synergistic quantification.

Synergy doesn't need to be the highest ideal, it's simply a math game. Does this synergistic approach produce more value than this automated approach? "Value" of course doesn't simply mean value in terms of dollars and cents. If you're making money in the short term but burning customer loyalty, you're just borrowing money from a bankrupt future.

PROCESSES AND DOCUMENTATION

BUSINESS PROCESSES ARE AT THE CENTER OF THE SEVENTH PRINCIPLE. As you build integrated marketing components it's absolutely essential that you create standard operating procedures that lend themselves to the development, maintenance and management of these components over the long term. Integration without applied process can't scale properly and to its full potential because it hasn't been appropriately identified or documented.

Further, when you integrate systems without a process or documentation in place, you put yourself at risk for future errors and issues. As your campaign continues to grow, you'll begin adding more tools and technologies to your toolset. If you haven't outlined and documented the integration procedures you've followed, you'll continuously be forced to reverse engineer each of your integrated components in an attempt to determine how a workflow is constructed to build in your new tools.

In the development world, we call this spaghetti code. It's aptly named as it simply means that your application is so messy in terms of how it interfaces with the various components that make up its whole, that any changes force you to try and unravel a bowl of spaghetti.

Think about workflow integrations as being as simple as how information passes between a landing page and the CRM, what connectors are used and how something may be tagged. None of these processes is earth shattering but they can all have massive implications to the future abilities of an integrated process if you don't remember to account for them when you make future changes.

When you add marketing automation to the discussion, the danger multiplies on an exponential scale. Catalytic processes exist that, if misunderstood or forgotten, can send contacts into eternal cycles or rabbit holes or, maybe worse, force a drop off completely so they aren't found or registered.

Don't be afraid of integrating your utilities or campaigns. Simply make it a habit to document that integration in a way that allows you to quickly and easily identify the workflow for each component. There's no "right way" to document integration because it's so vastly different depending upon your needs and purposes.

I wish I could offer you up a spreadsheet with a basic "here's how we do it" breakdown. Sadly, that doesn't exist. Every Client has their own needs and deployed tool sets so every system of documentation is completely different and based upon the needs of the Client. In some cases the best forms of documentation are housed within the tools instead of as a separate document. However, in the cases of extremely robust campaigns you will absolutely need a summary document that illustrates how all of the tools function together.

As an example of "in app" documentation: if you're building a form that will ultimately trigger an automated process, somewhere in the name or description of that form, make sure you indicate what process is triggered, what connectors are being used, the actual sequence being triggered (so you can find it easily) and where the sequence is housed. That might look something like this:

TRIGGERS AUTOMATION: Zapier > Mailchimp—SEQUENCE: "PPC Audit—thank you and follow up"

The nomenclature you use is completely up to you and should be revised to suit your business needs. However, as you'll see in the example above, someone completely unfamiliar with the campaign could very easily lift the hood and know exactly what's going on, where to begin their troubleshooting in the event of a problem, and what the next step in the sequence is.

I have yet to encounter a tool that doesn't allow for some level of custom naming or notation that I can use to help document the processes in place. The benefit of documenting your processes within the tool is that it doesn't provide or create an extra layer of work. You're simply describing what's happening with each new step in your build out as you do the work.

Getting company buy-in and enforcing the practice on standard operating procedures like this one is absolutely essential. One rogue employee who gets lazy or apathetic can cause a world of confusion if s/he ignores these requirements. This is true for the creation of campaign elements as well as for any changes made to them.

One of the major benefits of documenting your workflow is that you'll be creating functional standard operating procedures for future Clients. While every Client's integration needs are going to be different, you'll find that there are facets and sections that can be taken directly from existing Client campaigns. Instead of having to work through the integration and workflow anew, you now have the ability of offering up a case study and a documented workflow to follow, step by step.

Documentation of processes allows you to create blueprints for entire business models. You're building out the workflow to your lead intake, process management, data collection & reporting and a limitless amount of other potential processes that didn't exist before you created them. When you integrate tools, you're creating a solution. While that solution may not be proprietary to you it still has an immense amount of value as an offering since you're developing a connection where one didn't exist previously.

Pro Tip: Within the workflow management of your documentation I would recommend always including the unique identifiers necessary to understand how profiles, tools and utilities are connected. If someone has to pick up with the management of a campaign where you or a member of your team left off, it's helpful to know the user ID or account name of the various tools you used if you have multiple accounts. This will ensure no one is sent off on a wild goose chase attempting to track all that information down. I would also recommend investing in an account management tool like lastpass.com, passpack.com or splikity.com.

Your documented integration will also yield a visual roadmap of potential improvements. As you review your documentation you'll of course be able to see what processes you have already built but it can just as easily highlight processes that are missing. If you have excellent processes for lead intake developed and then have separate processes for post-purchase nurture created, you'll find yourself drawn to the gap between the two. This is an excellent opportunity to build a lead management and segmentation process that bridges that gap.

Don't make the documentation of processes out to be more than it is. This isn't a topic that should scare you away, nor is it something that you're going to have to learn how to do. Think of it as a stick figure narrative that tells the story of your marketing campaign. You've more than likely drawn out the workflow of a marketing funnel or email nurture before and this is no more complex than that. It's just a living version of your marketing campaign that exists so that everyone involved knows exactly what the workflow looks like. If you have used lucid chart or something similar, try and build a visual representation of each step of your campaign. Boom, you're documented.

Pardon me while I derail the conversation for a short Mr. Rogers moment. The documentation of your processes and methods is an extremely valuable knowledge base of information. One of the risks you run when you begin to utilize pre-built processes for new Clients, is the need to disclose these processes to the Client. I have seen agencies in the past withhold this information from Clients after the engagement was terminated.

While there are differing views as to what is right and wrong, you should be compelled to share what's reasonable within the confines of functional management, meaning that your Client needs to know how to properly manage their campaigns and administer all the technology you have incorporated without you, if ever necessary. Leaving them without that knowledge is unethical in my opinion. In most cases this means making your process management and documentation available to them and their team. I realize this is a tough pill to swallow, but I think the conversation is worth having. An ethical code of conduct is an important part of any industry.

Not providing your process documentation to a Client can be akin to not providing the admin credentials to a website that you've built them. They've paid for the pieces which means they deserve to know how to run the whole. You don't necessarily have to train them on how you would use it if that's what you choose to do; you do, however, need to put them in the position of being able to operate the mechanism.

TECHNICAL INTEGRATION

TECHNICAL INTEGRATION SHOULD BECOME A SECOND LANGUAGE TO YOU and your marketing team. Attempting to build out multi-faceted marketing campaigns and relying on manual processes dilutes your value, forces you and your team to spend time on unnecessary and trivial assignments and slows your ability to grow. Review your manual processes and look to identify areas for automation and integration to give you the opportunity to spend your time on tasks that will have a tangible long-term impact.

The vast majority of available tools offer some level of integration. As discussed already, your tool choices should be predicated on their ability to integrate with the applications that make up your core foundation whenever possible. Find synergistic tool sets to amplify the value of your time. For example, assume that part of your integrated digital marketing campaign on behalf of a Client included regular content creation for their blog. When you write a new blog you also include that blog in an email blast to subscribers who have expressed interest in that topic. Additionally, you post the new blog to your social channels.

Performing each of these tasks manually isn't difficult from a technical perspective. Once the content is written the distribution channels above are all relatively simple to use assuming your templates are created, segments assigned and processes written. They're so simple in fact that this is a task I would normally trust to a Virtual Assistant if I wasn't able to automate it. However, that's still an issue. Even if you have a VA working on a campaign, you need to catalyze the process, manage the workflow and perform quality assurance on the work.

VAs are cheaper than in-house employees but they still account for an additional cost and the propensity for human error is typically higher. In addition, chances are your work will be entered into a queue and will need to wait for completion until they're available. If you're not using a VA and you're attempting to do this yourself or through a member of your staff, then the cost of the process increases proportionately. Something as simple as a blog post ends up being a process and could potentially eat away an hour or two of someone's day.

However, every one of these processes can be completely automated. When you post a new blog to WordPress you can build an automated mechanism using a myriad of available tools (Mailchimp, Aweber, Feedburner, etc.) that will automatically notify your subscribers of the new post. Additionally, there are quite a few plugins (many of them free) that allow you to automatically post website updates to all of your social channels. Through WordPress you can even schedule your new post so that the email and social posts happen at whatever you deem to be the best day and time.

Through a small and relatively simple integration, you've taken a manual process and automated it in a way that allows you to focus on more important action items. This is one example of a limitless number of options. I'd strongly recommend looking at tools like Zapier, itDuzzit, IFTTT and Center, to see what types of available integrations exist for tools that you're already using. In addition, it might even be worth looking at your legacy tools and seeing if there are integrations available for them that you weren't aware of or have been added since you started using them.

You should already be familiar with the myriad of tools available that are built around the concept of automating digital processes. These are tools like Infusionsoft, HubSpot, Pardot, Eloqua, SharpSpring, Marketo, and a host of others too numerous to name. These applications can act as the foundation of your digital marketing initiatives by driving, managing and catalyzing your digital marketing processes.

NEEDLE MOVER TASKS VS. ROCK MOVER TASKS

A ROCK MOVER TASK IS A TASK THAT ACCOMPLISHES A NECESSARY BUT mundane activity. Rock mover tasks are usually tasks that can be accomplished by virtual assistants or interns. They're low skill, sometimes tedious tasks that are necessary to a marketing campaign but not necessarily worthy of your time.

A needle mover task is a task that drives a level of performance or improvement that will yield long-term and potentially exponential results. When you've successfully "moved the needle" you're yielding value and creating output. This is where your time should be spent as a digital marketer.

The more that you can automate your rock mover tasks, the more time you'll have to dedicate to needle mover tasks. In an interesting turn of irony, building the automation mechanism to complete a rock mover task is a needle mover task. Once the mechanism is built it will yield value that exceeds the time invested.

In some cases, you aren't able to automate rock mover tasks. There might be technical limitations that inhibit your ability to automate your task or needs that require manual oversight. In the cases where you're unable to build a true technical integration, you should still focus on building processes that increase the speed and efficiency with which the task is accomplished.

Even though certain processes require manual intervention, that doesn't mean that they can't be streamlined. I usually refer to any system of manual automation as a tickler system. Using the same example of the blog post we spoke about earlier, we would build a manual process that would catalyze each of the subsequent steps using manual "ticklers" to see the task streamlined to completion.

The blog template document that the writer uses would include a submission procedure that s/he would have to fill out and complete before marking the task as "complete." This submission is the "tickler" to the person in charge of posting and will catalyze their posting, on-site optimization and quality assurance of the post. In the posting SOP, they would be required to submit the completed blog link to the email marketing team and the social media marketing team prior to being able to have the blog signed off on.

You can see how these processes can carry on in perpetuity. The creation of the manual process ensures that each of the necessary tasks is properly accomplished and saves you or your project managers from constantly having to create and manage repetitive tasks every time a new blog is written.

AUTOMATION

I COULD WRITE AN ENTIRE BOOK ON AUTOMATION. I'M SURE THAT MAKES you hurt just to think about. Marketing automation is one of the great new frontiers of our industry and something about which I'm exceptionally passionate. The ability for automation to scale our value is next to limitless and something I would advise very strongly you spend some time learning and incorporating into your skill set.

Automation is far too robust a topic to attempt a comprehensive overview of without diving deeper than our specific needs call for. However, I saved automation for the end of this book due to its immense importance. Now that you have learned the 7 Critical Principles of Effective Digital Marketing, I would strongly recommend your next educational journey be in the realm of automation. For now, I'd like to cover the principles of automation as they relate to digital marketing and, more specifically, how to scale a campaign.

The very first thing to know when discussing automation is that we should always test first and automate second. Automation without proof of concept is a waste. Before you spend the time to automate a process you need to run the process manually and validate your assumptions. In many cases this might have already been done through the creation of processes and procedures. All of your existing SOPs can be considered "validated" and are easily something you can move to automate.

However, when you're building a new campaign for a Client, automation should not be the very first consideration. Before we automate, we need to prove concept and, until the assumptions we make are validated, automation shouldn't be something that we plan for. Even after a process or assumption has been tested and proven viable, you'll need to examine the benefits to automating over handling the process manually. While automation more often than not makes sense, in some cases the workload required to automate a process may exceed the benefits.

No matter what you choose to automate (or which tools you automate with), you'll need to incorporate the ability to house manual processes within your automated workflow. While there are marketing campaigns, Client nurture campaigns, process workflows and fulfillment procedures that can be 100% automated, more often you'll find yourself with a hybrid campaign that requires a combination of automated and manual procedures.

Your manual procedures need to live within your automated procedures without interrupting the automated workflow. In fact, the ideal scenario would be for manual procedures to continue to cata-

217

lyze further automation within the system. Applications like Infusionsoft, Salesforce and HubSpot have tool sets available to build in this type of manual process inclusion within your automated workflows. In other instances, where the tool set isn't explicitly available, you'll need to construct your own processes that ensure any manual processes continue to allow the automated workflow to fulfill its stated goal, depending upon how the manual process results.

One of the best examples I have of this is in sales automation. You can very easily automate hundreds of customer touch points using emails, SMS messages and social outreach. However, at some point you may want to trigger a task for a sales person to reach out directly to a prospect. Sometimes this happens after a prospect does something to qualify themselves, other times it's simply good form to begin a human to human connection. Either way, this type of process can't become an "end point" in your automation. Instead, it needs to be an integrated component.

Making manual processes a part of your global automation will help you to scale to a much larger degree than attempting to separate the two entirely. There's no clear line of demarcation any longer. The separation between automation and manual completion has blurred past the point of being able to completely delineate the two. Don't limit yourself by trying to draw a line in the sand between where your automation ends and your manual processes begin.

This isn't just true for sales and marketing. It's equally as important in process and workflow management. There are always going to be cases in the completion of a specific process where there has to be manual intervention or assistance. This can be in cases of quality assurance, scoping of new projects or customized pricing. Regardless of the instance, allowing automation to continue after manual intervention will further quantify your ability to scale.

In some instances, you may find yourself in a position where the manual processes need to serve as the catalyst and even set the ongoing pace of further optimization. Using the sales process as an example again, you may find it necessary to deliver automated communication that aligns with the phase of the buying cycle that a salesperson indicates a prospect is in. Make sure that your automation mechanisms allow for this type of dual-pronged approach. Your automation should be able to trigger and/or guide manual processes just as easily as your manual processes should be able to catalyze and guide your automation.

APPLICATION SUGGESTIONS

1. Take Inventory of Your Integration Map

Spend some time looking at the tools you're already using and review their available integrations. Almost all the SAAS tools available on the market today will have a dedicated library of available tools with which they integrate. More often than not these integrations are built with their core user needs in mind. This means that the integrations typically speak to a common issue, requirement or value-add that their user base requested. It stands to reason that, since you're using the tool, you may have similar needs.

The tools that are available on an integration list can also be looked at as a type of preferred partner for the tool you're already using. Creating a short list for future toolset expansion should be done with these "recommended tools" in mind if not completely from this paradigm. The ability to integrate with tools that you're already using and happy with is an excellent benefit. An added benefit is the fact that the tool you like, know and trust would appear to like, know and trust some of these recommended tools.

In many cases, you may find yourself with multi-dimensional integration capabilities. This means that you have three or more apps that all integrate with each other in various ways. While this is an excellent position to be in, you'll want to make sure that you map out how you intend to integrate and potentially automate any processes. You may run into logical errors or redundancies that need to be worked out before an integration can be completed.

Just because an integration is available now doesn't mean you need to take advantage of it. However, I do believe you should understand what each of your tools allows from an integration standpoint. This knowledge will arm you in the future as you build out Client campaigns and encounter new need requirements that may change the existing paradigm you have in place.

I would also highly recommend reviewing the available connectors for the applications that you're using. Tools like Zapier and IFTTT are great at building out integrations between multiple apps and toolsets. However, just because a tool integrates with Zapier doesn't mean that it necessarily does what you want/need from an integration standpoint. Zapier does a good job at outlining what types of triggers and data swaps are possible between tools. Make sure to review that prior to banking on the ability to build a plug and play solution with a connector.

2. Ask for the Integrations You Would Like to See

Good SAAS companies listen! And the ones that don't won't be around very long. I have yet to encounter a digital tool that didn't have a type of mechanism that allowed for me to request/suggest a new type of functionality or feature. Sometimes you'll find that the request is already on their roadmap for completion.

I can't count the number of times a new functionality or feature has been added or fast tracked simply because I took the time to ask about it. The features or integrations you request are only going to make their tool stronger and more valuable to future users. It also doesn't hurt to follow up every now and again about features that are on the development road map. As with all things, the squeaky wheel gets the oil.

In many cases, you may find yourself with the opportunity to be a beta user for new functionality. Quite a few tools utilize their power users and more active Clients to test new functionality before rolling it out to everyone. This will give you the unique opportunity of being far ahead of the curve with toolsets that could have dramatic impacts on your marketing campaigns. Be careful about how you use these tools, of course. Beta users are testing an application for bugs so I wouldn't recommend putting a high-risk campaign on a beta tool.

Work to communicate and build a relationship with the providers of your core tools. If you'll take a small amount of time to invest in providing them with feedback, offering suggestions and even allowing them to use you as a resource, you'll begin to find that your ability to influence the direction of the tool increases dramatically.

3. Automate the Easy Things First Just to Get into the Habit

Building automation is a daunting task. All too often I see newly inducted automators attempt to build out automated workflows for core business processes only to find themselves overwhelmed by an endless iterative cycle of second guessing, backtracking and stagnation. Start with some quick and small wins and work to build automation into your business processes slowly. Not only will this be much easier and faster, it'll also prove to be a stronger foundation for the long term. Simple automation tends to be much stronger than complex automated workflows.

For example, you probably have a regular weekly (monthly, quarterly, whatever) meeting with your staff. Automate the meeting updates, reminders and follow ups. This isn't going to change the face of your business but it will allow you to play with automation in a way that doesn't risk driving you insane but also provides some value and allows you to start building an automated shop.

Once you have a simple automated workflow in place, start to expand on it. Using the example above, you can include the regular itinerary (if there is one) and links to resources that should be referenced in the meeting. You can request attendance confirmation and automate a post-meeting survey.

This slow and steady approach will result in automated workflows that are extremely well vetted and of immense value. They'll also give you the opportunity to learn the tools and proficiencies necessary in a safe environment before you start putting them to work on Client campaigns. You'll also start to build a portfolio of automated tools that you can use as examples and even case studies when you speak to new prospects about automation.

10

SOOOOO... NOW WHAT?

Now that you have read my book and you know the 7 Critical Principles of Effective Digital Marketing, you are officially a super supreme ninja digital marketing badass. You will never encounter another digital marketing problem again and all digital marketing campaigns you run will kneel before you in passive compliance as you bulldoze your way to success, nerd-fame and fortune.

Or...

This isn't the end. In fact, there is no end. That's a little depressing, isn't it? There's not a principle presented in this book that will lead you to anything that will ever resemble an end point. Each of the core principles we have discussed is meant to spur growth and catalyze future learning. If anything, I just created more work for you. However, I hope that I have provided a construct that allows you to focus that future work in a way that is more targeted, productive and rewarding.

My sincere (and possibly arrogant) hope would be that you don't leave this behind as another book read and another checkbox checked. Instead, try to use this as an ongoing resource throughout your digital marketing journey. Reference it when you encounter specific issues and work to build your business around the 7 Principles in a way that makes them a part of you and your company's professional DNA.

Incidentally, I'm allowed to say all of this because, as stated in the beginning, I didn't invent any of this. I simply compiled this information over years of study, pulled it together in a simple and extremely entertaining format and now profit greatly from my theft. I hope that you profit equally from having read this and taking the principles and building them into the core foundation of your digital marketing paradigm.

I'm also of the strong opinion that this isn't a book that should only be read once. We all experience cycles of learning. These cycles equip us with the ability to learn more from situations and resources than we might have been prepared to do prior to entering the new cycle. As you grow in your business and practice, revisit this as a growth resource and make a concerted effort to ensure that these principles continue to stay infused into your upward scale.

I believe that you'll continue to benefit from revisiting this book because you'll be reading it from an entirely new context each time. The application of the information is heavily contextualized against your current state and situation. As those states and situations change, so does the way you intake and apply new data. With each new stage of growth, revisit this book! You'll find that doing so not only helps ensure that you're on the right track, but it also helps to aim future growth and align ongoing business with the core principles.

If you're interested in continuing to learn about *The 7 Critical Principles of Effective Digital Marketing,* sign up for my newsletter: kasim.me/connect. You'll get regular updates with valuable content surrounding these concepts.

A PERSONAL NOTE

Thank you. Sincerely and from the bottom of my heart, thank you for buying this, reading it and coming on this little journey with me. *[Unless you didn't buy it. If you somehow stole it then I retract my thanks and replace it with a magnanimous and lacking all semblance of humility, "You're Welcome". I hope you learned something. Chief among the things that I hoped you learn is not to steal, you dick. Unless you came across this for free in a legitimate fashion. Then I'm sorry I just called you a dick. I hope we can still be friends.]*

Jokes aside, I'm truly grateful to be in the position I'm in right now. At present and for reasons that I'm still never 100% sure are entirely legitimate, I'm someone you're willing to listen to. That just tickles me pink. I have the sad and pathetic personality trait that seeks out attention and validation. I've stopped trying to fight it and simply embrace it as part of who I am. This book, as you can imagine, plays pretty strongly into that personality flaw and I appreciate your helping to contribute to my weaknesses.

I actually have a really big favor to ask of you. Can you please hop online and write a review about this book? Amazon.com and goodreads.com are my primary targets but beggars can't be choosers and I'll take what I can get. Social proof is so insanely valuable for an initiative like this one. I'm sorry if you think this request is in poor taste. I just worked so hard on this thing and I'd like to do everything I can to get the word out there.

Even if you don't feel up for writing a review (sniff, sniff) I would love to hear your feedback! Give me the good and the bad. I know my writing style can be frustrating and I have a penchant for wordiness. I'd love to receive as much constructive criticism as you have to offer. This is a growth exercise for me as well and the more honesty I'm afforded, the better I'll be with the next book I write! So, if you have something to say please don't hesitate to email me at: me@kasim.me.

I want everything you're willing to throw at me—thoughts, opinions, disagreements, etc. I want it all! Please don't hold back. I would also love to hear about any gaps you believe existed and if there were any topics I might have missed or glazed over. This will help arm me for the next book I attempt. Speaking of which…

If you're interested in getting a sneak peak at my next project (and maybe even a free copy if you're open to being an advanced reader) then don't forget to subscribe to my newsletter! Just visit this link: kasim.me/connect.

So, thank you again dear reader. I can't begin to tell you what this opportunity has meant to me. I'm thrilled at the ability to have engaged you on some small level and hope very sincerely that you feel as though the time you have invested has been worth it. I wish you the best in your future digital marketing endeavors and hope that you don't hesitate to share with others what you have learned here.

I hope we're given the opportunity to meet at some point in the future. I'll let you buy me a drink and we can talk about how humble I am.

Sincerely,

Kasim Aslam

Made in the USA
Lexington, KY
16 February 2018